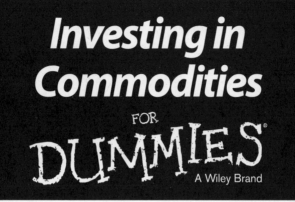

Investing in Commodities

FOR

DUMMIES®

A Wiley Brand

by Amine Bouchentouf

Investing in Commodities **For Dummies®**

Published by: **John Wiley & Sons, Inc.,** 111 River Street, Hoboken, NJ 07030-5774, www.wiley.com

Copyright © 2016 by John Wiley & Sons, Inc., Hoboken, New Jersey

Published simultaneously in Canada

For general information on our other products and services, please contact our Customer Care Department within the U.S. at 877-762-2974, outside the U.S. at 317-572-3993, or fax 317-572-4002. For technical support, please visit www.wiley.com/techsupport.

Wiley publishes in a variety of print and electronic formats and by print-on-demand. Some material included with standard print versions of this book may not be included in e-books or in print-on-demand. If this book refers to media such as a CD or DVD that is not included in the version you purchased, you may download this material at http://booksupport.wiley.com. For more information about Wiley products, visit www.wiley.com.

Library of Congress Control Number: 2015951693

ISBN 978-1-119-12201-2 (pbk); ISBN 978-1-119-12203-6 (ePub); ISBN 978-1-119-12202-9 (ePDF)

Manufactured in the United States of America

10 9 8 7 6 5 4 3 2 1

Contents at a Glance

Table of Contents

Introduction

*W*hy are commodities, long regarded as an inferior asset class, quickly moving to the investing mainstream? Good performance. Investors like to reward good performance, and commodities have performed well in recent years. In addition, investors can more easily access these markets: Plenty of new investment vehicles, from exchange-traded funds (ETFs) to master limited partnerships (MLPs), have been introduced to satisfy investor demand.

As commodities have been generating more interest, there's a large demand for a product to help average investors get a grip on the market fundamentals. Commodities as an asset class have been plagued by a lot of misinformation, and it's sometimes difficult to separate fact from fiction or outright fantasy. The aim of *Investing in Commodities For Dummies* is to help you figure out what commodities are all about and, more important, develop an intelligent investment strategy to profit in this market. Of course, as with every other asset class, commodities are subject to market swings and disruptions, which can be a source of risk but also an opportunity. As the 2008 Global Financial Crisis demonstrated, even the savviest investors with the latest up-to-date market information can struggle with unique investment events.

These disruptions are part of the market process. Investors who protect themselves through a "margin of safety" philosophy will be able to protect their downside during periods of extreme volatility. Using this book, you'll better equip yourself to avoid the pitfalls inherent in any investment activity.

About This Book

My aim in writing *Investing in Commodities For Dummies* is to offer you a comprehensive guide to the commodities markets and show you a number of investment strategies to help you profit in this market. You don't have to invest in just crude oil or gold futures contracts to benefit. You can trade ETFs, invest in companies that process commodities such as uranium, buy precious metals ownership certificates, or invest in master limited partnerships. The commodities markets are global in nature, and so are the investment opportunities. My goal is to help you uncover these global opportunities and offer you investment ideas and tools to unlock and unleash the power of the commodities markets. Best of all, I do all of this in plain English!

Anyone who's been around commodities, even for a short period of time, realizes that folks in the business are prone to engage in linguistic acrobatics. Words like *molybdenum, backwardation,* and *contango* are thrown around like "hello" and "thank you." Sometimes these words seem intimidating and confusing. Don't be intimidated. Language is powerful, after all, and getting a grip on the concepts behind the words is critical, especially if you want to come out ahead in the markets. That's why I use everyday language to explain even the most abstract and arcane concepts.

Icons Used in This Book

One of the pleasures of writing a *For Dummies* book is that you get to use all sorts of fun, interactive tools to highlight or illustrate a point. Here are some icons that I use throughout the book:

I use this icon to highlight information that you want to keep in mind or that's referenced in other parts of the book.

When you see this icon, make sure that you read the accompanying text carefully: It includes information, analysis, or insight that will help you successfully implement an investment strategy.

I explain more technical information with this icon. The commodities markets are complex, and the vocabulary and concepts are quite tricky. You can skip these paragraphs if you just want a quick overview of the commodities world, but be sure to read them before seriously investing. They give you a better grasp of the concepts discussed.

Investing can be an extremely rewarding enterprise, but it can also be a hazardous endeavor if you're not careful. I use this icon to warn you of potential pitfalls. Stay alert for these icons because they contain information that may help you avoid losing money.

Beyond the Book

In addition to all the material you can find in the book you're reading right now, this product also comes with some access-anywhere goodies on the web. Check out the eCheat Sheet at www.dummies.com/cheatsheet/investing incommodities for helpful insights and details about the benefits of diversification, how to decipher public disclosure forms, and the major influencer of oil markets.

Where to Go from Here

I've organized this book in a way that gives you the most accurate and relevant information related to investing in general and commodity investing in particular. The book is modular in nature, meaning that although it reads like a book from start to finish, you can read one chapter or even a section at a time without needing to read the whole book to understand the topic that's discussed.

If you're a true beginner, however, I recommend that you read Parts I and II carefully before you start skipping around in the chapters on particular commodities.

Part I
Just the Facts on Commodities

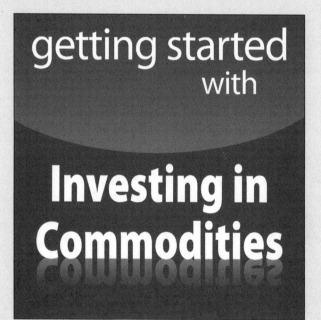

getting started
with

Investing in Commodities

In this part . . .

✔ Know why you should invest in commodities, check out the commodities markets, and find the best ways to invest in commodities

✔ Celebrate the advantages, acknowledge the downsides, and manage risk when investing in commodities

Chapter 1

Investors, Start Your Engines! An Overview of Commodities

. . . .

In This Chapter

▶ Finding out why you should invest in commodities

▶ Defining the commodities markets

▶ Determining the best ways to trade commodities

▶ Identifying the major commodities

. . . .

*T*he commodities markets are broad and deep, presenting both challenges and opportunities. Investors are often overwhelmed simply by the number of commodities out there: more than 30 tradable commodities to choose from. (I cover almost all of them — 32, to be exact — more than any other introductory book on the topic.) How do you decide whether to trade crude oil or gold, sugar or palladium, natural gas or frozen concentrated orange juice, soybeans or aluminum? What about corn, feeder cattle, and silver — should you trade these commodities as well? And if you do, what's the best way to invest in them? Should you go through the futures markets, go through the equity markets, or buy the physical stuff (such as silver coins or gold bullion)? And do all commodities move in tandem, or do they perform independently of each other?

With so many variables to keep track of and options to choose from, just getting started in commodities can be daunting. Have no fear — this book provides you with the actionable information, knowledge, insight, and analysis to help you grab the commodities market by the horns. You've maybe heard a lot of myths and fantasies about commodities. I shatter some of these myths and, in the process, clear the way to help you identify the real money-making opportunities.

For example, a lot of folks equate (incorrectly) commodities exclusively with the futures markets. Undoubtedly, the two are inextricably linked — the futures markets offer a way for commercial users to hedge against commodity price risks and a means for investors and traders to profit from this price risk. However, the futures market is only one planet in the commodities universe.

The equity markets are also involved in commodities. Companies such as ExxonMobil (NYSE: XOM) focus on the production of crude oil, natural gas, and other energy products; Anglo-American PLC (NASDAQ: AAUK) focuses on mining precious metals and minerals across the globe; and Starbucks (NASDAQ: SBUX) offers investors access to the coffee markets. Ignoring these companies that process commodities isn't only narrow minded, but it's also a bit foolish because they provide exposure to the very same commodities traded on the futures market.

In addition to the futures and equity markets, a number of investment vehicles allow you to access the commodities markets. These vehicles include master limited partnerships (MLPs), exchange-traded funds (ETFs), and commodity mutual funds (all covered in Chapter 12). So although I do focus on the futures markets, I also examine investment opportunities in the equity markets and beyond.

The commodities universe is large, and investment opportunities abound. In this book, I help you explore this universe inside and out, from the open outcry trading pits on the floor of the New York Mercantile Exchange to the labor-intensive cocoa fields of the Ivory Coast; from the vast palladium-mining operations in northeastern Russia to the corn-growing farms of Iowa; from the Ultra Large Crude Carriers that transport crude oil across vast oceans to the nickel mines of Papua New Guinea; from the sugar plantations of Brazil to the steel mills of China.

By exploring this fascinating universe, not only do you get insight into the world's most crucial commodities — and get a glimpse of how the global capital markets operate — you also see how to capitalize on this information to generate profits.

Defining Commodities and Their Investment Characteristics

Just what, exactly, are commodities? Put simply, commodities are the raw materials humans use to create a livable world. Humans have been exploiting earth's natural resources since the beginning of time. They use agricultural products to feed themselves, metals to build weapons and tools, and energy to sustain themselves. Energy, metals, and agricultural products are the three classes of commodities, and they are the essential building blocks of the global economy.

For the purposes of this book, I present 32 commodities that fit a very specific definition, which I define in the following bulleted list. For example, the commodities I present must be raw materials. I don't discuss currencies — even though they trade in the futures markets — because they're not a raw material; they can't be physically used to build anything. In addition, the commodities must present real moneymaking opportunities to investors.

All the commodities I cover in the book have to meet the following criteria:

- ✓ **Tradability:** The commodity has to be tradable, meaning that there needs to be a viable investment vehicle to help you trade it. For example, I include a commodity if it has a futures contract assigned to it on one of the major exchanges, if a company processes it, or if an ETF tracks it.

  Uranium, which is an important energy commodity, isn't tracked by a futures contract, but several companies specialize in mining and processing this mineral. By investing in these companies, you get exposure to uranium.

- ✓ **Deliverability:** All the commodities have to be physically deliverable. I include crude oil because it can be delivered in barrels, and I include wheat because it can be delivered by the bushel. However, I don't include currencies, interest rates, and other financial futures contracts because they're not physical commodities.

- ✓ **Liquidity:** I don't include any commodities that trade in illiquid markets. Every commodity in the book has an active market, with buyers and sellers constantly transacting with each other. Liquidity is critical because it gives you the option of getting in and out of an investment without having to face the difficulty of trying to find a buyer or seller for your securities.

Going for a Spin: Choosing the Right Investment Vehicle

The two most critical questions to ask yourself before getting started in commodities are the following: What commodity should I invest in? How do I invest in it? I answer the second question first and then examine which commodities to choose.

The futures markets

In the futures markets, individuals, institutions, and sometimes governments transact with each other for price-hedging and speculating purposes. An airline company, for instance, may want to use futures to enter into an agreement with a fuel company to buy a fixed amount of jet fuel for a fixed price for a fixed period of time. This transaction in the futures markets allows the airline to hedge against the volatility associated with the price of jet fuel. Although commercial users are the main players in the futures arena, traders and investors also use the futures market to profit from price volatility through various trading techniques.

One such trading technique is *arbitrage,* which takes advantage of price discrepancies between different futures markets. For example, in an arbitrage trade, you purchase and sell the crude oil futures contract simultaneously in different trading venues, for the purpose of capturing price discrepancies between these venues.

The futures markets are administered by the various commodity exchanges, such as the Chicago Mercantile Exchange (CME) and the Intercontinental Exchange (ICE). I discuss the major exchanges, the role they play in the markets, and the products they offer in Chapter 13.

The most direct way of investing in the futures markets is to open an account with a *futures commission merchant* (FCM). The FCM is much like a traditional stock brokerage house (such as Schwab, Fidelity, or Merrill Lynch), except that it's allowed to offer products that trade on the futures markets. Here are some other ways to get involved in futures:

- ✔ **Commodity trading advisor (CTA):** The CTA is an individual or company licensed to trade futures contracts on your behalf.

- ✔ **Commodity pool operator (CPO):** The CPO is similar to a CTA, except that the CPO can manage the funds of multiple clients under one account. This pooling provides additional leverage when trading futures.

- ✔ **Commodity indexes:** A commodity index is a benchmark, similar to the Dow Jones Industrial Average or the S&P 500, that tracks a basket of the most liquid commodities. You can track the performance of a commodity index, which allows you to essentially "buy the market." A number of commodity indexes are available, including the Goldman Sachs Commodity Index and the Reuters/Jefferies CRB Index, which I cover in Chapter 12.

These examples are only a few ways to access the futures markets. Be sure to read Chapters 11 and 12 for additional methods.

A number of organizations regulate the futures markets, including the Securities and Exchange Commission (SEC) and the Commodity Futures Trading Commission (CFTC). These organizations monitor the markets to prevent market fraud and manipulation and to protect investors from such activity. Check out Chapter 13 for an in-depth analysis of the role these regulators play and how to use them to protect yourself from market fraud.

Trading futures isn't for everyone. By their very nature, futures markets, contracts, and products are extremely complex and require a great deal of mastery by even the most seasoned investors. If you don't feel that you have a good handle on all the concepts involved in trading futures, don't simply jump into futures — you could lose a lot more than your principal (because of the use of leverage and other characteristics unique to the futures markets). If you're not comfortable trading futures, don't sweat it. You can invest in commodities in multiple other ways.

The equity markets

Although the futures markets offer the most direct investment gateway to the commodities markets, the equity markets also offer access to these raw materials. You can invest in companies that specialize in the production, transformation, and distribution of these natural resources. If you're a stock investor familiar with the equity markets, this may be a good route for you to access the commodities markets. The only drawback of the equity markets is that you have to take into account external factors, such as management competence, tax situation, debt levels, and profit margins, which have nothing to do with the underlying commodity. That said, investing in companies that process commodities still allows you to profit from the commodities boom.

Publicly traded companies

The size, structure, and scope of the companies involved in the business are varied, and I cover most of these companies throughout the book. I offer a description of the company, including a snapshot of its financial situation, future growth prospects, and areas of operation. I then make a recommendation based on the market fundamentals of the company.

You encounter these types of companies in the book:

- ✔ **Diversified mining companies:** A number of companies focus exclusively on mining metals and minerals. Some of these companies, such as Anglo-American PLC (NASDAQ: AAUK) and BHP Billiton (NYSE: BHP), have operations across the spectrum of the metals complex, mining metals that range from gold to zinc. I look at these companies in Chapter 9.

- ✔ **Electric utilities:** Utilities are an integral part of modern life because they provide one of life's most essential necessities: electricity. They're also a good investment because they have historically offered large dividends to shareholders. Read Chapter 5 to figure out whether these companies are right for you.

- ✔ **Integrated energy companies:** These companies, such as ExxonMobil (NYSE: XOM) and Chevron (NYSE: CVX), are involved in all aspects of the energy industry, from the extraction of crude oil to the distribution of liquefied natural gas (LNG). They give you broad exposure to the energy complex (see Chapter 6).

This list is only a small sampling of the commodity companies I cover in these pages. I also analyze highly specialized companies, such as coal-mining companies (Chapter 5), oil refiners (Chapter 6), platinum-mining companies (Chapter 7), and purveyors of gourmet coffee products (Chapter 10).

Master limited partnerships

Master limited partnerships (MLPs) invest in energy infrastructure such as oil pipelines and natural gas storage facilities. I'm a big fan of MLPs because they're a *publicly traded partnership.* They offer the benefit of trading like a corporation on a public exchange, while offering the tax advantages of a private partnership. MLPs are required to transfer all cash flow back to shareholders, which makes them an attractive investment. I dissect the structure of MLPs in Chapter 12 and introduce you to some of the biggest names in the business so you can take advantage of this unique investment.

Managed funds

Sometimes it's just easier to have someone else manage your investments for you. Luckily, you can count on professional money managers who specialize in commodity trading to handle your investments.

Consider a few of these options:

- ✔ **Exchange-traded funds (ETFs):** ETFs are an increasingly popular investment because they're managed funds that offer the convenience of trading like stocks. In recent years, a plethora of ETFs has appeared to track everything from crude oil and gold to diversified commodity indexes. Find out how to benefit from these vehicles in Chapter 12.

- ✔ **Mutual funds:** If you've previously invested in mutual funds and are comfortable with them, look into adding a mutual fund that gives you exposure to the commodities markets. A number of funds are available that invest solely in commodities. I examine these commodity mutual funds in Chapter 12.

If you have a pet or a child, sometimes you hire a pet sitter or babysitter to look out after your loved ones. Before you hire this individual, you interview candidates, check their references, and examine their previous experience. When you're satisfied with the top candidate's competency, only then do you entrust that person with the responsibility of looking after your cat, daughter, or both. The same thing applies when you're shopping for a money manager, or money sitter. If you already have a money manager you trust and are happy with, stick with him. If you're looking for a new investment professional to look after your investments, you need to investigate him as thoroughly as possible. In Chapter 14, I examine the selection criteria to use when shopping for a money manager.

Physical commodity purchases

The most direct way of investing in certain commodities is to actually buy them outright. Precious metals such as gold, silver, and platinum are a great example of this. As the price of gold and silver has skyrocketed recently, you may have seen ads on TV or in newspapers from companies offering to buy your gold or silver jewelry. As gold and silver prices increase in the futures markets, they also cause prices in the spot markets to rise (and vice versa). You can cash in on this trend by buying coins, bullion, or even jewelry. I present this unique investment strategy in Chapter 7.

This investment strategy is suitable for only a limited number of commodities, mostly precious metals like gold, silver, and platinum. Unless you own a farm, keeping live cattle or feeder cattle to profit from price increases doesn't make much sense. And I won't even mention commodities like crude oil or uranium!

Checking Out What's on the Menu

I cover 32 commodities in the book. Here's a listing of all the commodities you can expect to encounter while going through these pages. (Although the book is modular in nature, I list the commodities here in order of their appearance in the text.)

Energy

Energy has always been indispensable for human survival and also makes for a great investment. Energy, whether fossil fuels or renewable energy sources, has attracted a lot of attention from investors as they seek to profit from the world's seemingly unquenchable thirst for energy. I present in this book all the major forms of energy, from crude oil and coal to electricity and solar power, and show you how to profit in this arena.

- **Crude oil:** Crude oil is the undisputed heavyweight champion in the commodities world. More barrels of crude oil are traded every single day (87 million and growing) than any other commodity. Accounting for 40 percent of total global energy consumption, coal provides some terrific investment opportunities.

- **Natural gas:** Natural gas, the gaseous fossil fuel, is often overshadowed by crude oil. Nevertheless, it's a major commodity in its own right, used for everything from cooking food to heating houses during the winter. I also take a look at the prospects of liquefied natural gas (LNG).

- **Coal:** Coal accounts for more than 20 percent of total world energy consumption. In the United States, the largest energy market, 50 percent of electricity is generated through coal. Because of abundant supply, coal is making a resurgence.

- **Uranium/nuclear power:** Because of improved environmental standards within the industry, nuclear power use is on the rise. I show you how to develop an investment strategy to capitalize on this trend.

- **Electricity:** Electricity is a necessity of modern life, and the companies responsible for generating this special commodity have some unique characteristics. I examine how to start trading this electrifying commodity.

- **Solar power:** For a number of reasons that range from environmental to geopolitical, demand for renewable energy sources such as solar power is increasing.

- **Wind power:** Wind power is getting a lot of attention from investors as a viable alternative source of energy.

- **Ethanol:** Ethanol, which is produced primarily from corn or sugar, is an increasingly popular fuel additive that offers investment potential.

Other commodities are in the energy complex, such as heating oil, propane, and gasoline. Although I do provide insight into some of these other members of the energy family, I focus a lot more on the resources in the previous list.

Metals

Metallurgy has been essential to human development since the beginning of time. Societies that have mastered the production of metals have been able to thrive and survive. Similarly, investors who have incorporated metals into their portfolios have been able to generate significant returns. I cover all the major metals, from gold and platinum to nickel and zinc.

- **Gold:** Gold is perhaps the most coveted resource on the planet. For centuries, people have been attracted to its quasi-indestructibility and have used it as a store of value. Gold is a good asset for hedging against inflation and also for asset preservation during times of global turmoil.

- **Silver:** Silver, like gold, is another precious metal that has monetary applications. The British currency, the pound sterling, is still named after this metal. Silver also has applications in industry (such as electrical wiring) that places it in a unique position of being coveted for both its precious metal status and its industrial uses.

- **Platinum:** Platinum, the rich man's gold, is one of the most valuable metals in the world, used for everything from jewelry to the manufacture of catalytic converters.

- **Steel:** Steel, which is created by alloying iron and other materials, is the most widely used metal in the world. Used to build everything from cars to buildings, it's a metal endowed with unique characteristics and offers good investment potential.

- **Aluminum:** Perhaps no other metal has the versatility of aluminum; it's lightweight yet surprisingly robust. These unique characteristics mean that it's a metal worth adding to your portfolio, especially because it's the second most widely used metal (right behind steel).

- **Copper:** Copper, the third most widely used metal, is the metal of choice for industrial uses. Because it's a great conductor of heat and electricity, its applications in industry are wide and deep, making this base metal a very attractive investment.

- ✔ **Palladium:** Palladium is part of the platinum group of metals, and almost half of the palladium that's mined goes toward building automobile catalytic converters. As the number of cars with these emission-reducing devices increases, the demand for palladium will increase as well, making this an attractive investment.

- ✔ **Nickel:** Nickel is a ferrous metal that's in high demand because of its resistance to corrosion and oxidation. Steel is usually alloyed with nickel to create stainless steel, which ensures that nickel will play an important role for years to come.

- ✔ **Zinc:** The fourth most widely used metal in the world, zinc is sought after for its resistance to corrosion. It's used in galvanization, in which zinc coating is applied to other metals, such as steel, to prevent rust.

Agricultural products

Food is the most essential element of human life, and the production of food presents solid money-making opportunities. In this book you find out how to invest in the agricultural sector in everything from coffee and orange juice to cattle and soybeans:

- ✔ **Coffee:** Coffee is the second most widely produced commodity in the world, in terms of physical volume, behind only crude oil. Folks love a good cup of coffee, and this provides good investment opportunities.

- ✔ **Cocoa:** Cocoa production, which is dominated by a handful of countries, is a major agricultural commodity, primarily because it's used to create chocolate.

- ✔ **Sugar #11:** Sugar is a popular food sweetener, and it can be a sweet investment as well. Sugar #11 represents a futures contract for global sugar.

- ✔ **Sugar #14:** Sugar #14 is specific to the United States and is a widely traded commodity.

- ✔ **Frozen concentrated orange juice — type A:** FCOJ-A, for short, is the benchmark for North American orange juice prices because it's grown in the hemisphere's two largest regions: Florida and Brazil.

✔ **Frozen concentrated orange juice — type B:** FCOJ-B, like FCOJ-A, is a widely traded contract that represents global orange juice prices. This contract gives you exposure to orange juice activity on a world scale.

✔ **Corn:** Corn's use for culinary purposes is perhaps unrivaled by any other grain, which makes this a potentially lucrative investment. Check out Chapter 10.

✔ **Wheat:** According to archaeological evidence, wheat was one of the first agricultural products grown by man. It's an essential staple of human life and makes for a great investment.

✔ **Soybeans:** Soybeans have many applications, including as feedstock and for cooking purposes. The soybean market is a large market and presents some good investment opportunities.

✔ **Soybean oil:** Soybean oil, also known as vegetable oil, is derived from actual soybeans. It's used for cooking purposes and has become popular in recent years with the health-conscious dietary movement.

✔ **Soybean meal:** Soybean meal is another derivative of soybeans that's used as feedstock for poultry and cattle. It may not sound sexy, but it can be a good investment.

✔ **Live cattle:** For investors involved in agriculture, using the live cattle futures contract to hedge against price volatility is a good idea.

✔ **Feeder cattle:** Whereas the live cattle contract tracks adult cows, the feeder cattle contract hedges against the risk associated with growing calves. The markets don't widely follow this area, but it's important to figure out how this market works.

✔ **Lean hogs:** They may not be the sexiest commodity out there, but lean hogs are an essential commodity, making them a good trading target.

✔ **Frozen pork bellies:** Frozen pork bellies are essentially nothing more than good old bacon. This industry is cyclical and subject to wild price swings, which provides unique arbitrage trading opportunities.

Chapter 2

The Pros and Cons of Commodities

In This Chapter

▶ Examining strong reasons to consider commodities

▶ Acknowledging the inherent downsides

▶ Managing risk when investing in commodities

C ommodities have traditionally been considered the black sheep in the family of asset classes; for several decades, no respectable money manager wanted anything to do with them. This traditional lack of interest (which no longer applies, by the way) has generated a lot of misinformation about commodities. As a matter of fact, probably no other asset class has suffered through so much misunderstanding and misconception.

Many investors are scared of venturing into the world of commodities. For one thing, it seems that every time the word *commodities* is uttered, someone pops up with a horrible story about losing their entire life savings trading soybeans, cocoa, or some other exotic commodity. Even though this negative perception is rapidly changing, commodities are still often misunderstood as an investment. I actually know some investors who invest in commodities (and who have made money off them) but who don't understand the fundamental reasons commodities are such a good long-term investment.

In this chapter, I show you why commodities are an attractive investment and why many investors are becoming more interested in this asset class. Then again, I believe that many investors are afraid of commodities because they don't know much about them. My further aim in this chapter is to shed some light on the issues surrounding commodities so that you can invest with confidence. I'm not denying that commodities present some risk — all investments do. And so I give you some tools to minimize and manage those risks.

Why the 21st Century Is the Century of Commodities

Since autumn 2001, commodities have been running faster than the bulls of Pamplona. The Reuters/Jefferies CRB Index (a benchmark for commodities) nearly doubled between 2001 and 2006. During this period, oil, gold, copper, and silver hit all-time highs (although not adjusted for inflation). Other commodities also reached levels never seen before in trading sessions.

Many investors wondered what was going on. Why were commodities doing so well when other investments, such as stocks and bonds, weren't performing? I believe that we're witnessing a long-term cyclical bull market in commodities. Because of a number of fundamental factors (which I go through in the following sections), commodities are poised for a rally that will last well into the 21st century — and possibly beyond that. It's a bold statement, I know. But the facts are there to support me.

Although I'm bullish on commodities for the long term, I have to warn you that at times commodities won't perform well at all. This statement is simply the nature of the commodity cycle. Furthermore, in the history of Wall Street, no asset has ever gone up in a straight line. Minor (and, occasionally, major) pullbacks always happen before an asset makes new highs — if, in fact, it does make new highs.

Consider an example. During the first few months of 2006, commodities outperformed every asset class, with some commodities breaking record levels. Gold and copper both hit a 25-year high. Then during the week of May 15, commodities saw a big drop. The Reuters/Jefferies CRB Index fell more than 5 percent that week, with gold and copper dropping 10 and 7 percent, respectively.

Many commentators went on the offensive and started bashing commodities. "We are now seeing the beginning of the end of the rally in commodities," said one analyst. A newspaper ran the headline "Is This the End of Commodities?" An endless number of commentators hit the airwaves claiming that this was a speculative bubble about to burst. A respected economist even compared what was happening to commodities to the dotcom bubble: "There is no fundamental reason why commodity prices are going up." Nothing could be further from fact. A couple weeks after this minor pullback, some of these commodities that were being compared to highly leveraged tech stocks had regained most, if not all, of their lost ground. Even after the GFC, most commodities are now back to their precrisis levels, with many others making all-time highs.

There's a story behind the rise in commodities — and it's a pretty compelling one.

Ka-boom! Capitalizing on the global population explosion

The 21st century is going to experience the largest population growth in the history of humankind. The United Nations (UN) estimates that the world will add a little less than 1 billion people during *each* of the first five decades of the 21st century. The global population will grow to about 9 billion people by 2050 (as of 2015, approximately 7.3 billion people live on the planet).

Also consider the following statistic: According to the UN, the average number of years it takes to add 1 billion people has shrunk from an average of 130 years in the 19th century to approximately 13 years in the 21st century! The rate at which the human population is increasing has reached exponential levels.

So how is this relevant to commodities? Put simply, significant population growth translates into greater global demand for commodities. Humans are the most voracious consumers of raw materials on the planet — and the only ones who pay for them. As the number of humans in the world increases, so will the demand for natural resources. After all, people need food to eat, houses to live in, and heat to stay warm during the winter — all of this requires raw materials. This large population growth is a key driver for the increasing demand for commodities, which will continue to put upward pressure on commodity prices.

Profiting from urbanization

Perhaps even more significant than population growth is the fact that it's accompanied by the largest urbanization movement the world has ever seen. In the early 20th century, according to the UN, less than 15 percent of the world's population lived in cities; by 2005, that number jumped to 50 percent — and still shows no sign of decreasing. As a matter of fact, 60 percent of the world's population is expected to live in urban areas by the year 2030.

Urbanization is highly significant for commodities because people who live in urban centers consume a lot more natural resources than those who live in rural areas. In addition, more natural resources are required to expand the size of cities as more people move to them (rural to urban migration) and have more kids (indigenous urban population growth). More natural resources are required for the roads, cars, and personal appliances that are staples of city life.

Industrial metals such as copper, steel, and aluminum are going to be in high demand to construct apartment buildings, schools, hospitals, cars, and so on. So investing in industrial metals is one possible way to play the urbanization card. Be sure to read Chapter 8 for more information on these metals.

Benefiting from industrialization

The first industrial revolution, which took place in the 19th century, was a major transformational event primarily confined to Western Europe and North America. Major industrialization didn't spread to other corners of the globe until parts of the 20th century — even then, it was only sporadic.

A new wave of industrialization is taking place in the 21st century, and it may be the most important one in history. This wave is transforming a large number of developing countries into more industrialized countries, and raw materials are fueling this transformation.

Although many developing countries are on the fast track to industrialization, four countries need to be singled out as the frontrunners in this movement — Brazil, Russia, India, and China. They're collectively known as the *BRIC countries,* or just the BRICs.

The BRIC countries, which are now on a path toward full industrialization, are scouring the globe to secure supplies of key natural resources such as oil, natural gas, copper, and aluminum — the raw materials necessary for a country to industrialize.

As demand from the BRIC countries for natural resources increases, expect to see increasing upward price pressures on commodities.

What Makes Commodities Unique

As an asset class, commodities have unique characteristics that separate them from other asset classes and make them attractive, whether as independent investments or as part of a broader investment strategy. I go through these unique characteristics in the following sections.

Gaining from inelasticity

In economics, *elasticity* seeks to determine the effects of price on supply and demand. The calculation can get pretty technical, but, essentially, elasticity quantifies how much supply and demand will change for every incremental change in price.

Goods that are elastic tend to have a high correlation between price and demand, which is usually inversely proportional: When prices of a good increase, demand tends to decrease. This relationship makes sense because you're not going to pay for a good that you don't need if it becomes too expensive. Capturing and determining that spread is what elasticity is all about.

Inelastic goods, however, are goods that are so essential to consumers that changes in price tend to have a limited effect on supply and demand. Most commodities fall in the inelastic goods category because they're essential to human existence.

For instance, if the price of ice cream increased by 25 percent, chances are, you'd stop buying ice cream. Why? Because it's not a necessity, but more of a luxury. However, if the price of unleaded gasoline at the pump increased by 25 percent, you definitely wouldn't be happy about the price increase, but you'd still fill up your tank. The reason? Gas is a necessity — you need to fill up your car to go to work or school, run errands, and so on.

The demand for gasoline isn't absolutely inelastic, however — you won't keep paying for it regardless of the price. A point will come at which you'd decide that it's simply not worth it to keep paying the amount you're paying at the pump, so you'd begin looking for alternatives. (Read Chapter 5 for more information on alternative energy sources.) But the truth remains that you're willing to pay more for gasoline than for other products you don't need (such as ice cream); that's the key to understanding price inelasticity.

Most commodities are fairly inelastic because they're the raw materials that allow us to live the lives we strive for; they help us maintain a decent (and, in some cases, extravagant) standard of living. Without these precious raw materials, you wouldn't be able to heat your home in the winter — actually, without cement, copper, and other basic materials, you wouldn't even have a house to begin with! And then there's the most essential commodity of all: food. Without food, we wouldn't exist.

Because of the absolute necessity of commodities, you can be sure that as long as there are humans around, there's going to be a demand for these raw materials.

Finding a safe haven

During times of turmoil, commodities tend to act as safe havens for investors. These investors view certain commodities, such as gold and silver, as reliable stores of value, so they flock to these assets when times aren't good. When currencies slide, nations go to war, or global pandemics break out, you can rely on gold, silver, and other commodities to provide you with financial safety.

For example, after the horrible acts of September 11, 2001, the price of gold jumped as investors sought safety in the metal.

 It's a good idea to have part of your portfolio in gold and other precious metals so that you can protect your assets during times of turmoil. Turn to Chapter 7 for more on investing in precious metals.

Hedging against inflation

One of the biggest factors to watch out for as an investor is the ravaging effects of inflation. Inflation can devastate your investments, particularly paper assets such as stocks. The central bankers of the world — smart people all — spend their entire careers trying to tame inflation, but despite their efforts, inflation can easily get out of hand. You need to protect yourself against this economic enemy.

Ironically, one of the only asset classes that *benefits* from inflation is, you guessed it, commodities. Perhaps the biggest irony of all is that increases in the prices of basic goods (commodities such as oil and gas) actually contribute to the increase of inflation.

For example, there's a positive correlation between gold and the inflation rate. During times of high inflation, investors load up on gold because it's considered a good store of value.

Taking time to bring new sources online

The business of commodities is a time- and capital-intensive business. Unlike investments in high-tech companies or other "new economy" investments (such as e-commerce), bringing commodity projects online takes a lot of time.

For example, it can take up to a decade to bring new sources of oil online. First, a company must identify potentially promising areas to explore for oil. After locating an area, the company has to actually start drilling and prospecting for the oil. If it's lucky, this process of discovering significantly recoverable sources of oil takes only three to five years. The company must then develop infrastructure and bring in machinery to extract the oil, which must be transported to a refining facility to be transformed into consumable energy products such as gasoline or jet fuel. After it goes through the lengthy refining stage, the end product must finally be transported to consumers.

So what does this all mean to you as an investor? When you're investing in commodities, you have to think long term! If you're used to investing in tech stocks or if you're an entrepreneur involved in e-commerce, you need to radically change the way you think about investing when you approach commodities. If you're able to recognize the long-term nature of commodities, you'll be on your way to becoming a successful commodities investor.

Sell in May and go away? Definitely nay!

You may have heard the saying "Sell in May and go away." This is a Wall Street adage referring to stocks. The thinking goes that because the stock market doesn't perform well during the summer months, you should sell your stocks and get back into the game in the fall.

This adage doesn't apply to commodities because commodities move in different cycles than stocks. Some commodities perform really well during the summer months. For example, because summer is the heavy driving season, there's an increase in demand for gasoline products. Thus, all things equal, unleaded gasoline tends to increase in price during the summer.

I discuss the cyclical nature of commodities in the following section.

Commodities and the Business Cycle

Commodities are cyclical in nature. Returns on commodity investments aren't generated in a vacuum — they're influenced by a number of economic forces. In other words, the performance of commodities, like that of other major asset classes, is tied to general economic conditions. Because economies move in cycles, constantly alternating between expansions and recessions, commodities react according to the current economic phase.

The performance of commodities as an asset class is going to be different during economic expansions than during recessions.

As a general rule, commodities tend to do well during periods of late expansions and early recessions. The reason is that, as the economy slows, key interest rates are decreased to stimulate economic activity — this tends to help the performance of commodities. Stocks and bonds, on the other hand, don't perform as well during recessions. As an investor seeking returns across all phases of the business cycle, opening up to commodities enables you to generate returns during good and bad economic times.

The study of cycles, whether for commodities, stocks, or other assets, isn't an exact science. I don't recommend using cycles as the foundation of a trading or investment strategy. Instead, try to use the study of cycles to get a sense of what historical patterns have indicated — and where an asset class is heading.

Although the historical pattern of commodities tends to show better performance during late expansions and early recessions, this in no way guarantees that commodities will keep following this pattern. Actually, during the latest commodity bull market, commodities have acted independently of the business cycle. This performance may be attributed to the fact that, for the reasons outlined in the section "Why the 21st Century Is the Century of Commodities," this commodity bull market is a different beast than in previous cycles.

The Pitfalls of Using Leverage

In finance, *leverage* refers to the act of magnifying returns through the use of borrowed capital. Leverage is a powerful tool that gives you the opportunity to control large market positions with relatively little upfront capital. However, leverage is the ultimate double-edged sword because both your profits and losses are magnified to outrageous proportions.

If you invest in stocks, you know that you're able to trade on margin. You have to qualify for a margin account, but when you do, you're able to use leverage (margin) to get into stock positions. You can also trade commodities on margin. However, the biggest difference between using margin with stocks and using margin with commodities is that margin requirement for commodities is much lower than margins for stocks, which means the potential for losses (and profits) is much greater in commodities.

If you qualify for trading stocks on margin, you need to have at least 50 percent of the capital in your account before you can enter into a stock position on margin.

The minimum margin requirements for commodity futures vary but, on average, are lower than those for stocks. For example, the margin requirement for soybeans in the Chicago Board of Trade is 4 percent. This means that, with only $400 in your account, you can buy $10,000 worth of soybeans futures contracts! If the trade goes your way, you're a happy camper. But if you're on the losing side of a trade on margin, you can lose much more than your principal.

Another big difference between stock and commodity futures accounts is that the balance on futures accounts is calculated at the end of the trading session. So if you get a margin call, you need to take care of it immediately.

When you're trading on margin, which is essentially trading on borrowed capital, you may get a margin call from your broker requiring you to deposit additional capital in your account to cover the borrowed amount.

Because of the use of margin and the extraordinary amounts of leverage you have at your disposal in the futures markets, you need to be extremely careful when trading commodity futures contracts. To be a responsible investor, I recommend using margin only if you have the necessary capital reserves to cover any subsequent margin calls you may receive if the market moves adversely.

Understanding the Real Risks behind Commodities

Investing is all about managing the risk involved in generating returns. In this section, I lay out some common risks you face when investing in commodities and some small steps you can take to minimize these risks.

Sovereign government risk

In the era following the 2008 credit crisis, a more acute risk emerged: the sovereign government risk. This type of risk is more important than other types of risks because it involves the balance sheet of sovereign governments. During the financial crisis, banks were in a position to bail out consumers; when banks started to fail, governments began to bail out the banks. However, when governments start to fail, few institutions can bail them out.

This type of risk became more evident in the European countries, accustomed to single-digit gross domestic profit (GDP) growth rates and relaxed lifestyles due to generous government programs and pensions. For a number of reasons (geographic, demographic, and economic), these countries no longer enjoy the place in the sun they once occupied, which is leading to the risk that these states may start defaulting. In addition to liquidity risks, these states pose a solvency risk — in other words, they simply cannot pay back their borrowers.

Many countries in Europe, such as Greece, Portugal, Spain, Ireland, and, to some extent, Italy and France (Germany being the main exception) — are facing severe budget cuts and unprecedented decreases in government expenditure programs. This situation has caused riots and violence across Europe. As their unfavorable demographic trends further accelerate and their manufacturing base is eroded by more competitive spheres in Asia and other emerging markets, expect to see more belt-tightening in Europe in the coming years. In a post-2008 world, it's necessary to carefully examine the countries you're investing in.

Geopolitical risk

One of the inherent risks of commodities is that the world's natural resources are located on various continents, and the jurisdiction over these commodities lies with sovereign governments, international companies, and many other entities. For example, to access the large deposits of oil located in the Persian Gulf region, oil companies have to deal with the sovereign countries of the Middle East that have jurisdiction over this oil.

Negotiations for natural resource extractions can get pretty tense pretty quickly, with disagreements arising over licensing agreements, tax structures, environmental concerns, employment of indigenous workers, access to technology, and many other complex issues.

International disagreements over the control of natural resources are common. Sometimes a host country simply kicks out foreign companies involved in the production and distribution of the country's natural resources. In 2006, Bolivia, which contains South America's second-largest deposits of natural gas, nationalized its natural gas industry and kicked out the foreign companies involved. In a day, a number of companies, such as Brazil's Petrobras and Spain's Repsol, were left without a mandate in a country where they had spent billions of dollars developing the natural gas industry. Investors in Petrobras and Repsol paid the price.

So how do you protect yourself from this geopolitical uncertainty? Unfortunately, you can't wave a magic wand to eliminate this type of risk. However, one way to minimize it is to invest in companies with experience and economies of scale. For example, if you're interested in investing in an international oil company, go with one that has an established international track record. A company like ExxonMobil, for instance, has the scale, breadth, and experience in international markets to manage the geopolitical risk it faces. A smaller company without this sort of experience faces more risk than a bigger one. In commodities, size does matter.

Speculative risk

Similar to the bond or stock markets, the commodities are populated by traders whose primary interest is making short-term profits by speculating whether the price of a security will go up or down.

Unlike commercial users who are using the markets for hedging purposes, speculators are simply interested in making profits; thus, they tend to move the markets in different ways. Although speculators provide much-needed liquidity to the markets (particularly in commodity futures markets), they tend to increase market volatility, especially when they begin exhibiting what former Federal Reserve Chairman Alan Greenspan termed "irrational exuberance." Because speculators can get out of control, as they did during the dotcom bubble, you need to always be aware of the amount of speculative activity going on in the markets. The amount of speculative money involved in commodity markets is in constant flux, but as a general rule, most commodity futures markets consist of about 75 percent commercial users and 25 percent speculators.

Although I'm bullish on commodities because of the fundamental supply-and-demand story, too much speculative money coming into the commodities markets can have detrimental effects. I anticipate that, at times, speculators will drive the prices of commodities beyond the fundamentals. If you see too much speculative activity, it's probably a good idea to simply get out of the markets.

If you trade commodities, constantly check the pulse of the markets; find out as much as possible about who the market participants are so that you can distinguish between the commercial users and the speculators. One resource I recommend is the Commitment of Traders report, put out by the Commodity Futures Trading Commission (CFTC). This report, available online at www.cftc.gov/cftc/cftccotreports. htm, gives you a detailed look at the market participants. For more information on the CFTC and other regulatory bodies, check out Chapter 13.

Corporate governance risk

As if you didn't have enough to worry about, you also need to watch out for plain and simple fraud. The CFTC and other regulatory bodies do a decent job of protecting investors from market fraud, but the possibility of becoming a victim of fraud does exist. For example, your broker may hide debts or losses in offshore accounts.

One way to prevent being taken advantage of is to be extremely vigilant about where you're putting your money. Thoroughly research a firm before you hand over your money. I go through the due diligence process to follow when selecting managers in Chapter 14. Unfortunately, sometimes no amount of research or due diligence can protect you from fraud — it's just a fact of the investment game.

Managing Risk

You cannot completely eliminate risk, but you can sure take steps to help you reduce it. In this section, I go through time-proven and market-tested ways to minimize risk.

Due diligence: Just do it

One way to minimize risk is to research all aspects of the investment you're about to undertake — before you undertake it. Too often, investors don't start doing research until after they invest in commodities contracts or companies.

Many investors buy on hype; they hear a certain commodity mentioned in the press, and they buy just because everyone else is buying. Buying on impulse is one of the most detrimental habits you can develop as an investor. Before you put your money into anything, you need to find out as much as possible about this potential investment.

Because you have a number of ways to invest in commodities (which I discuss in Chapter 11), the type of research you perform depends on the approach you take. The following sections go over the due diligence to perform for each investment methodology.

Commodity companies

One way to get exposure to commodities is to invest in companies that process commodities. Although this is an indirect way to access raw materials, it's a good approach for investors who are comfortable in the equity environment.

Ask a few questions before you buy the company's stock:

- ✔ What are the company's assets and liabilities?
- ✔ How effective is the management with the firm's capital?
- ✔ Where will the firm generate future growth?
- ✔ Where does the company generate its revenue?
- ✔ Has the company run into any regulatory problems in the past?
- ✔ What is the company's structure? (Some commodity companies are corporations, whereas others act as limited partnerships.)
- ✔ How does the company compare with competitors?
- ✔ Does the company operate in regions of the world that are politically unstable?
- ✔ What is the company's performance across business cycles?

Of course, this list gives only a few questions to ask before making an equity investment. I go through a series of other facts and figures to gather about commodity companies in Chapter 6 (for energy companies) and Chapter 9 (for mining companies).

You can get the answers to these questions by looking through the company's annual report (Form 10K) and quarterly reports (Form 8K).

Managed funds

If you're not a hands-on investor or you simply don't have the time to actively manage your portfolio, you may want to choose a manager to do the investing for you. You can choose from a number of different managers, including the following:

- ✔ **Commodity mutual fund:** Manager of mutual funds that invest in commodities
- ✔ **Commodity pool operator:** Manager of group futures accounts
- ✔ **Commodity trading advisor:** Manager of individual futures accounts

Before you invest with a manager, find out as much as you can about him. Ask a few questions:

- ✔ What is the manager's track record?
- ✔ What's his investing style? Is it conservative or aggressive, and are you comfortable with it?
- ✔ Does he have any disciplinary actions against him?
- ✔ What do clients have to say about him? (It's okay to ask a manager if you can speak to one of his existing clients.)
- ✔ Is he registered with the appropriate regulatory bodies? (Turn to Chapter 13 for information on the regulators.)
- ✔ What fees does he charge? (Ask whether some fees aren't disclosed: Always watch out for hidden fees!)
- ✔ How much in assets does he have under management?
- ✔ What are his after-tax returns? (Make sure that you specify *after*-tax returns, because many managers post returns only before taxes are considered.)
- ✔ Are minimum time commitments involved?
- ✔ Are penalties assessed if you choose to withdraw your money early?
- ✔ Are minimum investment requirements applied?

In Chapter 14, I go through other qualifying questions to ask before choosing a manager to invest money for you.

Futures market

The futures markets play an important role in the world of commodities. They provide liquidity and allow hedgers and speculators to establish benchmark prices for the world's commodities.

If you're interested in investing through commodity futures, you need to ask a lot of questions before you get started. Consider some of these questions:

- ✔ On what exchange is the futures contract traded?

- ✔ Is there an accompanying option contract for the commodity?

- ✔ Is the market for the contract liquid or illiquid? (You want it to be liquid, just in case you're wondering.)

- ✔ Who are the main market participants?

- ✔ What's the expiration date for the contract you're interested in?

- ✔ What's the open interest for the commodity?

- ✔ Are there any margin requirements? If so, what are they?

Commodity fundamentals

Whether you decide to invest through futures contracts, commodity companies, or managed funds, you need to gather as much information as possible about the underlying commodity itself. This caveat is perhaps the most important piece of the commodities puzzle because the performance of any investment vehicle you choose depends on the actual fundamental supply-and-demand story of the commodity.

Ask yourself a few questions before you start investing in a commodity, whether it's coffee or copper:

- ✔ Which country or countries hold the largest reserves of the commodity?

- ✔ Is the country politically stable, or is it vulnerable to turmoil?

- ✔ How much of the commodity is actually produced on a regular basis? (Ideally, you want to get data for the daily, monthly, quarterly, and annual basis.)

- ✔ Which industries or countries are the largest consumers of the commodity?

- ✔ What are the primary uses of the commodity?

✔ Are there any alternatives to the commodity? If so, what are they, and do they pose a significant risk to the production value of the target commodity?

✔ Do seasonal factors affect the commodity?

✔ What's the correlation between the commodity and comparable commodities in the same category?

✔ What are the historical production and consumption cycles for the commodity?

These questions are only a few to ask before you invest in any commodity. Ideally, you want to be able to gather this information before you start trading.

Diversify, diversify, diversify

One of the best ways to manage risk is to diversify. This strategy applies on a number of levels: both diversification *among* asset classes, such as bonds, stocks, and commodities; and diversification *within* an asset class, such as diversifying commodity holdings among energy and metals.

For diversification to have the desired effects on your portfolio (to minimize risk), you want to have asset classes that perform differently. One of the benefits of using commodities to minimize your overall portfolio risk is that commodities tend to behave differently than stocks and bonds. The performance of commodities and equities, for example, is remarkably different. This fact means that when stocks aren't doing well, you'll at least have your portfolio exposed to an asset class that is performing.

Part II
Making Money in Energy

Four Major Integrated Oil Companies

- ExxonMobil (ticker: XOM): 2015 revenues of $394 billion, earnings of $51 billion

- Chevron (ticker: CVX): 2015 revenues of $170 billion, earnings of $19 billion

- ConocoPhillips (ticker: COP): 2015 revenues of $165 billion, earnings of $7.5 billion

- Eni (ticker: E): 2015 revenues of $102 billion, earnings of $5.5 billion

Check out an article on peak oil at www.dummies.com/extras/investingincommodities.

In this part . . .

- ✔ Invest in oil, know about key metrics, brush up on market fundamentals, and invest in oil companies

- ✔ Understand the main uses of natural gas, figure out market signals, check out liquefied natural gas (LNG), and invest in natural gas companies and futures

- ✔ Examine renewable energy investing, including solar, wind, and biofuel, and check out coal, nuclear, and electricity

- ✔ Profit in investment in energy companies, from discoveries to refineries and shipping

Chapter 3

It's a Crude, Crude World: Investing in Crude Oil

• •

• •

*C*rude oil is undoubtedly the king of commodities, in both its production value and its importance to the global economy. Crude oil is the most-traded nonfinancial commodity in the world today, and it supplies 40 percent of the world's total energy needs — more than any other single commodity. Despite many calls to shift energy consumption toward more renewable energy sources, the crude reality is that petroleum products are still the dominant resource worldwide. In fact, to this day, more barrels of crude oil are traded daily (92 million barrels by 2015 figures) than any other commodity. Crude oil's importance also stems from the fact that it's the base product for a number of indispensable goods, including gasoline, jet fuel, and plastics.

Oil is truly the lifeblood of the global economy. Without it, the modern world would come to a screeching halt. Drivers wouldn't be able to drive their cars, ships would have no fuel to transport goods around the world, and airplanes would be grounded indefinitely.

Because of its preeminent role in the global economy, crude oil makes for a great investment. In this chapter, I show you how to make money investing in what is arguably the world's greatest natural resource. However, the oil industry is a multidimensional, complex business with many players that often have conflicting interests. Proceeding with a bit of caution and making sure that you understand the market fundamentals is essential for success.

In the following sections, I give you an overview of the global oil industry and the many links in the oil supply chain. I analyze consumption and production figures, introduce you to the major players (both countries and companies), and show you the best ways to execute a sound investment strategy.

Seeing the Crude Realities

Having a good understanding of the global consumption and production patterns is important if you're considering investing in the oil industry. Knowing how much oil is produced in the world, which countries are producing it, and which consumers are accepting the shipments allows you to develop an investment strategy that benefits from the oil market fundamentals.

I'm sometimes amazed at some of the misconceptions regarding the oil industry. For example, I was once speaking with students about energy independence and was shocked when a majority of them claimed that the United States got more than 50 percent of its oil from the Persian Gulf and Saudi Arabia, in particular; in fact, nothing could be farther from the truth.

The United States is the second-largest producer of crude oil in the world. Take a look at Table 3-2, and you'll quickly see that the United States produces more than 7 million barrels a day (this includes oil products), behind only Saudi Arabia and Russia. In fact, the United States didn't become a net importer of oil until 1993; until that point, the United States produced more than 50 percent of the oil it consumed domestically.

According to 2015 figures, the United States imports about 55 percent of its oil. If energy (oil) independence is measured by the percentage of oil a country imports, then the United States is more energy-independent than both Germany (which imports 80 percent of its oil) and Japan (which imports more than 90 percent).

The biggest oil exporter to the United States isn't a Middle
Eastern country, but our northern neighbor. That's right,
Canada is the largest exporter of crude oil to the United
States! Persian Gulf oil makes up about 20 percent of imported
oil to the U.S.

My point here is that a lot of misinformation about this topic
persists, and you need to be armed with the correct figures to
be a successful investor. In the following sections, I introduce
you to all the market participants (traders, major oil companies, and producing/consuming countries) and the metrics
they monitor, such as global reserve estimates, daily production rates, daily consumption rates, daily export figures, and
daily import figures. I present you with the most up-to-date
information regarding oil production and consumption patterns. Because these patterns are likely to change in the
future because of supply and demand, I also tell you where
you can go to get the latest information on the oil markets.
Having the facts makes you a better investor.

Examining global reserve estimates

As an investor, knowing which countries have large crude oil
deposits is an important part of your investment strategy.
As demand for crude oil increases, countries that have large
deposits of this natural resource stand to benefit tremendously. One way to benefit from this trend is to invest in
indigenous countries and companies with large reserves of
crude oil. (I go through this strategy in detail in the section
"Get your passport ready: Investing overseas," later in this
chapter.)

Oil & Gas Journal estimates that global proven crude oil
reserves as of 2015 are 1,342 billion barrels (1.34 trillion barrels). Table 3-1 lists the countries with the largest proven
crude oil reserves, according to 2010 data. These figures may
change as new oil fields are discovered, as new technologies
facilitate the extraction of additional oil from existing fields,
and as a result of natural depletion.

Table 3-1	Largest Oil Reserves by Country, 2015	
Rank	*Country*	*Proven Reserves (Billion Barrels)*
1	Saudi Arabia	261
2	Iran	150
3	Iraq	143
4	Kuwait	104
5	United Arab Emirates	99
6	Venezuela	98
7	Russia	60
8	Libya	41
9	Nigeria	36
10	United States	21

Source: Oil & Gas Journal

Although Canada isn't on this list, it has proven reserves of 4.7 billion barrels of *conventional* crude oil, which is crude that's easily recoverable and accounted for. In addition to conventional crude, Canada is rich in unconventional crude oil located in oil sands. Oil from oil sands is much more difficult to extract and, as a result, generally isn't included in the calculation of official and conventional reserve estimates. However, if Canada's oil sands were included, Canada would be catapulted to the number two spot, with a grand total of 178 billion barrels.

Having large deposits of crude doesn't mean that a country has exploited and developed all its oil fields. For example, although Iraq has the third-largest oil deposits in the world, it's not even among the top ten producing countries, because of poor and underdeveloped infrastructure. There's a big difference between proven reserves and actual production, as you can see by comparing Tables 3-1 and 3-2.

The calculation of proven, recoverable deposits of crude oil isn't an exact science. For example, *Oil & Gas Journal* figures are different from those of the Energy Information Administration (EIA), whose figures, in turn, are different from those of the International Energy Agency (IEA). I recommend taking a big-picture approach to global reserve estimates and consulting all the major sources for these statistics. To keep up on updated figures and statistics on the oil industry, check out the following organizations:

- ✔ **BP Statistical Review (BP):** www.bp.com
- ✔ **Energy Information Administration (EIA):** www.eia.doe.gov
- ✔ **International Energy Agency (IEA):** www.iea.org
- ✔ *Oil & Gas Journal:* www.ogj.com

Staying busy and productive: Looking at production figures

Identifying the countries with large reserves is important, but it's only a starting point as you begin investing in the oil markets. To determine which countries are exploiting these reserves adequately, I recommend looking at another important metric: actual production. Having large reserves is meaningless if a country isn't tapping those reserves to produce oil. Table 3-2 lays out the top ten producers of crude oil.

Table 3-2	Largest Producers of Crude Oil, 2015	
Rank	*Country*	*Daily Production (Million Barrels)*
1	Saudi Arabia	10.8
2	United States	10.5
3	Russia	10.2
4	Iran	4.2
5	China	4.0
6	Canada	3.4
7	Mexico	3.2
8	United Arab Emirates	3.0
9	Kuwait	2.8
10	Venezuela	2.6

Source: United States Department of Energy

A number of factors influence how much crude a country is able to pump out of the ground daily, including geopolitical stability and the application of technologically advanced crude-recovery techniques. Also remember that daily production may vary throughout the year because of disruptions resulting either from geopolitical events such as embargos, sanctions, and sabotage that put a stop to daily production or from other external factors, like weather. For example, consider Hurricane Katrina and its devastating effect on U.S. oil supply in summer 2005, as well as the BP Gulf oil spill in 2010.

You need to keep a close eye on global daily supply because any disruption in the production supply chain can have a strong impact on the current price of crude oil. Because there's a tight supply-and-demand equation, any disruption in supply can send prices for crude skyrocketing.

Traders in the commodity exchanges follow the daily crude oil production numbers closely. Benchmark crude oil contracts such as both the West Texas Intermediate (WTI), traded on the Chicago Mercantile Exchange (CME), and the North Sea Brent, traded on the Intercontinental Exchange (ICE) in London, are affected by supply numbers. As a result, the market closely watches any geopolitical event or natural disaster that may reduce production.

If you're an active oil trader with a futures account, following these daily production numbers — which are available through the Energy Information Administration (EIA) Web site, at www.eia.doe.gov — is crucial. The futures markets are particularly sensitive to daily crude oil production numbers, and any event that takes crude off the market can have a sudden impact on crude futures contracts. If you're a long-term investor in the markets, monitoring this number is also important because production figures can have an effect on the general stock market performance as well. For example, if rebels seize a pipeline in Nigeria and 300,000 barrels of Nigerian crude are taken off the market, this will result in higher crude prices, which will have an impact on U.S. stocks (they generally fall). Thus, your stock portfolio holdings may be at risk because of daily crude oil production disruptions. Therefore, monitoring this statistic regularly is important for both short-term traders and long-term investors.

It's a demanding field: Checking out demand figures

The United States tops the list of oil consumers and has been the single largest consumer of crude oil for the last 25 years. Although a lot of folks pay attention to the demand increase from China and India, most of the demand for crude oil (and the resulting price pressures) still comes from the United States. Traders around the world closely watch supply, but demand figures are equally important because they indicate a steady and sustained increase in crude demand for the mid- to long term. This is likely to maintain increased pressure on crude prices. I list the top ten consumers of crude oil in the world in Table 3-3.

Table 3-3	Largest Consumers of Crude Oil, 2015	
Rank	*Country*	*Daily Consumption (Million Barrels)*
1	United States	19.5
2	China	7.8
3	Japan	4.8
4	India	3.0
5	Russia	2.9
6	Germany	2.6
7	Brazil	2.5
8	Saudi Arabia	2.4
9	Canada	2.3
10	South Korea	2.2

Source: United States Department of Energy

As of 2015, global consumption stood at approximately 86 million barrels per day. The United States and China are currently the biggest consumers of crude oil in the world, and this trend will continue throughout the 21st century, with global consumption expected to increase to 120 million barrels a day by 2025. An important development to keep track of is that although global consumption figures might remain within a tight trading band, the consumer profile is likely to change. Specifically, you can expect oil consumption in OECD and developed countries to remain stagnant — and, in some cases, experience a decrease — and consumption in emerging market nations to increase. For example, the trend is for countries like China, India, Russia, and Saudi Arabia to continue to increase domestic consumption as their economies remain in a rapid growth trajectory. Countries that are fairly mature, such as Germany and Canada, won't experience growth nearly as fast as the emerging market economies.

Always design an investment strategy that will profit from long-term trends. This steady increase in global demand for crude oil is a good reason to be bullish on oil prices.

Going in and out: Eyeing imports and exports

When planning your investments in the oil market, another pair of numbers to keep close tabs on is export and import figures. Exports are different from production: A country can produce a lot of oil and consume most, if not all, of it — as the United States does. On the other end of the spectrum, a country can produce plenty of oil and export most of it, as is the case in the United Arab Emirates.

Identifying the top exporting countries allows you to zero in on the countries that are actually generating revenues from selling crude oil to other countries. Countries that are net exporters of crude stand to benefit tremendously from the oil boom, and you can get in on the action by investing domestically in these countries; I outline a strategy in the later section "Get your passport ready: Investing overseas." In Table 3-4, I list the top oil-exporting countries.

Traders pay a lot of attention to exports, but imports, which represent the other side of the equation, are equally important. Countries that are main importers of crude oil are primarily advanced, industrialized societies like Germany and the United States. These countries are rich enough that they can absorb crude oil price increases, but as a general rule, the importers face a lot of pressure during any price increases. This pressure sometimes translates into lower stock market performances in the importing countries, which means you need to be careful if you're exposed to the domestic stock markets of these oil importers. I list the top crude oil–importing countries in Table 3-5.

Table 3-4	Top Ten Oil Exporters, 2015	
Rank	**Country**	**Daily Oil Exports (Million Barrels)**
1	Saudi Arabia	8.1
2	Russia	7.1
3	United Arab Emirates	2.5
4	Iran	2.3
5	Norway	2.3
6	Kuwait	2.2
7	Nigeria	2.1
8	Venezuela	1.9
9	Algeria	1.8
10	Angola	1.7

Source: United States Department of Energy

Table 3-5	Top Ten Oil Importers, 2015	
Rank	**Country**	**Daily Oil Imports (Million Barrels)**
1	United States	1,012.2
2	Japan	4.9
3	China	3.7
4	Germany	2.3
5	South Korea	2.2
6	India	1.9
7	France	1.8
8	Spain	1.5
9	Italy	1.5
10	Taiwan	1.0

Source: United States Department of Energy

Going Up the Crude Chain

Crude oil by itself isn't very useful; it derives its value from its products. Only after it's processed and refined into consumable products such as gasoline, propane, and jet fuel does it become so valuable.

Crude oil was formed over millions of years from the remains of dead animals and other organisms whose bodies decayed in the earth. Because of a number of geological factors such as sedimentation, these remains were eventually transformed into crude oil deposits. Therefore, crude oil is literally a *fossil fuel* — a fuel derived from fossils. As a matter of fact, the word *petroleum* comes from the Latin words *petra,* which means "rock," and *oleum,* which means "oil." So the word *petroleum* literally means "oil from the rocks."

A barrel holds 42 gallons of crude oil or crude oil equivalents. (That's about 159 liters.) *Barrel* is abbreviated as *bbl, barrels* as *bbls.*

Not all crudes are created equal. If you invest in crude oil, you need to realize right off the bat that crude oil comes in different qualities with different characteristics. You'd be surprised by how different that "black stuff" can be from region to region. Generally, crude oil is classified into two broad categories: light and sweet, and heavy and sour. Other classifications are used, but these are the two major ones.

The two criteria most widely used to determine the quality of crude oil are density and sulfur content.

✔ **Density** usually refers to how much a crude oil yields in terms of products, such as heating oil and jet fuel. For instance, a crude oil with lower density, known as a *light crude,* tends to yield higher levels of products. On the other hand, a crude oil with high density, commonly referred to as a *heavy crude,* has lower product yields.

The density of a crude oil, also known as the *gravity,* is measured by a scale devised by the American Petroleum Institute (API). The higher the API number, expressed in degrees, the lower the density of the crude oil. Therefore, a crude oil with a density of 43 degrees API will yield more desirable crude oil products than a crude oil with a density of 35 degrees API. Heavy crude (which is found in Venezuela and Canada) has an API degree of 20 or below.

✔ **Sulfur content** is another key determinant of crude oil quality. Sulfur is a corrosive material that decreases the purity of a crude oil. Therefore, a crude oil with high sulfur content, which is known as *sour,* is much less desirable than a crude oil with low sulfur content, known as *sweet* crude.

How is this criteria important to you as an investor? First, if you want to invest in the oil industry, you need to know what kind of oil you're going to get for your money. If you're going to invest in an oil company, you need to be able to determine which type of crude it's processing. You can find this information in the company's annual or quarterly reports. A company involved in producing light, sweet crude will generate more revenue from this premium crude than one involved in processing heavy, sour crude. This distinction doesn't mean that you shouldn't invest in companies with exposure to heavy, sour crude; you just have to factor the type into your investment strategy.

Table 3-6 lists some important crude oils and their characteristics.

Table 3-6	Crude Oil Grades	
Crude Oil Type	**Density (API)**	**Sulfur Content**
North West Shelf (Australia)	60.0	0.01
Arab Super Light (Saudi Arabia)	50.0	0.06
Bonny Light (Nigeria)	35.4	0.14
Duri (Indonesia)	21.5	0.14

As you can see, you can choose from a wide variety of crude oil products as investments. If you're interested in investing in a specific country, you need to find out what kind of crude oil it produces. Ideally, you want a crude oil with low sulfur content and a high API number as a density benchmark.

Making Big Bucks with Big Oil

The price of crude oil skyrocketed during the first decade of the 21st century. If this period is any indication of what's in store for oil, you definitely want to develop a winning game plan to take advantage of this trend. That said, crude remains a volatile commodity that's subject to external market forces. Specifically, the Global Financial Crisis of 2008 and its aftermath resulted in a price collapse of global crude oil markets during that time period.

The period leading up to 2008 witnessed an overheating global economy, with excess liquidity, historically low interest rates, and increasing global trade. These forces (along with several others) pushed oil prices to their record highs, approaching $150 per barrel. However as the financial crisis struck Wall Street, Europe, and the rest of the world markets, oil prices experienced an asset price deflation similar to what most other assets were experiencing worldwide. Therefore, it's advisable to be mindful of economic forces operating outside internal market-specific considerations when trading oil markets. In other words, you must view spare capacity, production volumes, and other metrics inherent to the petroleum markets within the context of global market forces.

A lot of people are making a lot of money from the price fluctuations of crude and gasoline. Why shouldn't you be one of them? In this section, I show you how to actually profit from the prices at the pump!

Oil companies: Lubricated and firing on all cylinders

Oil companies get a bad rap. Whatever you may think of them, they make for a great investment. Oil companies are responsible for bringing precious energy products to consumers, and for this service they're compensated — handsomely. Oil companies are for-profit companies that are run for the benefit of their shareholders. Instead of complaining about oil companies, why not become a shareholder of one (or more)?

In this section, I talk about the integrated oil companies, sometimes known as "big oil," "the majors," or "integrated oil companies." These are the oil companies that are involved in all the phases of the oil-production process, from exploring for oil to refining it and then transporting it to consumers. ExxonMobil, Chevron Texaco, and BP are all "big oil" companies.

Big oil companies aren't the only players in the oil business. Many other companies are involved in specific aspects of the transformational process of crude oil. For example, some companies, like Valero, are primarily involved in refining; others, such as General Maritime, own fleets of tankers that transport crude oil and products. I discuss how to invest in these companies — the refiners, transporters, and explorers — in Chapter 6.

Flying solo: Looking at individual oil companies

The major oil companies have been posting record profits in recent years. In 2005, ExxonMobil announced the largest annual corporate profit in history as it earned a staggering $36.1 billion on revenues of $371 billion! To put it in perspective, Saudi Arabia's 2005 GDP was $338 billion. The company continued its record string of earnings, posting net income of $40.1 billion in 2007 and $45 billion in 2008. It went through a rough patch in 2009 with the Global Financial Crisis but still managed to earn more than $19 billion for the year. Another big oil company, ConocoPhillips (NYSE: COP), raked in $13.53 billion in profits for 2005, up 66 percent from the previous year. In 2009, ConocoPhillips posted net income of $4.8 billion. Meanwhile, Chevron Corp. posted $10.4 billion in net income for 2009.

These announcements are a result of the increased global demand for crude oil and its products, as well as the technological and managerial efficiency practiced by the majors. As global demand continues and supplies remain limited, I expect big oil companies to keep generating solid revenues and profits. As the Global Financial Crisis amply demonstrated, earnings and revenues don't move in a straight line; you need to be able to tactically position your portfolio to profit from short-term market disruptions. In Table 3-7, I list some of the companies you may want to include in your portfolio.

This table is only a brief snapshot of some of the major integrated oil companies you can choose to add to your portfolio. For a more comprehensive list, check out Yahoo! Finance's section on integrated oil companies, at `biz.yahoo.com/ic/120.html`.

Table 3-7	Major Integrated Oil Companies, 2015		
Oil Company	*Ticker*	*Revenues*	*Earnings*
ExxonMobil	XOM	$394 billion	$51 billion
Chevron	CVX	$170 billion	$19 billion
ConocoPhillips	COP	$165 billion	$7.5 billion
Eni	E	$102 billion	$5.5 billion

Most of these traditional oil companies have now moved into other areas in the energy sphere. These companies not only process crude oil into different products, but they also have vast petrochemicals businesses, as well as growing projects that involve natural gas and, increasingly, alternative energy sources. (To reflect this shift, for example, BP has changed its name from British Petroleum to Beyond Petroleum.) The bottom line is that investing in these oil companies gives you exposure to other sorts of products in the energy industry as well.

Although revenues and earnings are important metrics to look at before investing in these companies, you also need to perform a thorough due diligence that considers other important factors to determine a company's health. I introduce some of these key metrics in Chapter 6, to help you select the most suitable energy companies for your portfolio.

Oil company ETFs: Strength in numbers

If you can't decide which oil company you want to invest in, you have several other options that allow you to buy the market, so to speak. One option is to buy *exchange-traded funds* (ETFs) that track the performance of a group of integrated oil companies. I discuss ETFs in depth in Chapter 12, but here are a few oil company ETFs to consider:

- ✓ **Energy Select Sector SPDR (AMEX: XLE):** The XLE ETF is the largest energy ETF in the market. It's part of the S&P's family of *Standard & Poor's Depository Receipts* (SPDR), commonly referred to as *spiders,* and tracks the performance of a basket of oil company stocks. Some of the stocks it tracks include the majors ExxonMobil and Chevron; however, it also tracks oil services companies such as Halliburton and Schlumberger (which I discuss in Chapter 6). You get a nice mix of integrated oil companies and other independent firms by investing in the XLE.

✔ **iShares Goldman Sachs Natural Resources Sector (AMEX: IGE):** The IGE ETF mirrors the performance of the Goldman Sachs Natural Resources Sector index, which tracks the performance of companies like ConocoPhillips, Chevron, and BP, as well as refiners such as Valero and Suncor. (I talk about refiners in Chapter 6.) Although most of this ETF is invested in integrated oil companies, it also enables you to play a broad spectrum of energy companies.

✔ **iShares S&P Global Energy Sector (AMEX: IXC):** This ETF mirrors the performance of the Standard & Poor's Global Energy Sector index. Buying this ETF gives you exposure to companies such as ExxonMobil, Chevron, ConocoPhillips, and Royal Dutch Shell. Launched at the end of 2001, the ETF has 35 percent aggregate returns for a three-year period.

Get your passport ready: Investing overseas

Another great way to capitalize on oil profits is to invest in an emerging market fund that invests in countries that both sit on large deposits of crude oil and have the infrastructure in place to export crude oil.

A country may have large deposits of crude oil, but it isn't necessarily able to produce and export crude oil for a profit. Iraq is a good example. Even though it sits on the third-largest reserves of crude oil in the world (see Table 3-1), Iraq isn't even one of the top ten exporters of crude because its infrastructure and security environment isn't secure enough.

Countries that export crude oil have seen their current account surpluses reach record highs. (*Current account* measures a country's balance of payments as they relate to trade.) These windfall profits are having a tremendous effect on the economies of such countries. The stock markets of some of these countries, particularly the Persian Gulf countries (known as the *Gulf Cooperation Council,* or GCC), have had a remarkable run during the first decade of this century, averaging double-digit compounded annual returns. As their economies have grown from their hydrocarbon wealth, these countries have established sovereign wealth funds (SWFs) to diversify their earnings and holdings away from petroleum products.

Many Persian Gulf countries have large capital resources that they're deploying across global capital markets and asset purchases. Abu Dhabi, the city-state with the largest oil reserves in the United Arab Emirates, has established the Abu Dhabi Investment Authority (ADIA), the Abu Dhabi Investment Council (ADIC), and the International Petroleum Investment Corporation (IPIC) to invest its hydrocarbon receipts. This move has resulted in a broad and significant diversification of Abu Dhabi's economy away from petroleum and into other strategic sectors, such as technology and aerospace. The local stock markets are a great way to get exposure to these economies, and you can also follow private equity opportunities as an investor.

For the uninitiated, investing directly in emerging markets can be a risky proposition and requires a lot of research. Some countries have different regulatory rules than the United States, and you need to know those rules before you get involved in a foreign venture.

One way to play emerging markets while avoiding direct risks is to invest in emerging markets funds located in the United States. These funds hire professionals who are familiar with the business environment in target countries and can navigate these foreign investment seas. These funds enable you to take advantage of booms in foreign countries, while remaining within the safe regulatory and investing environment of the United States.

A couple emerging markets funds give you indirect exposure to the booming oil-exporting countries:

- ✔ Evergreen Emerging Markets Growth I (EMGYX)
- ✔ Fidelity Emerging Markets (FEMKX)

Chapter 4

Welcome to Gas Vegas! Investing in Natural Gas

● ●

In This Chapter

▶ Identifying the main uses of natural gas

▶ Taking a look at liquefied natural gas (LNG)

▶ Investing in natural gas companies and futures

● ●

*I*f crude oil is the king of commodities, natural gas is the queen. Although crude oil accounts for about 40 percent of total energy consumed in the United States (the biggest energy market in the world), approximately 25 percent of energy consumption comes from natural gas. Natural gas is therefore an important source of energy both in the United States and around the world, and it can offer tremendous moneymaking opportunities.

Similar to crude oil (see Chapter 3) and coal (see Chapter 5), natural gas is a *nonrenewable fossil fuel* found in large deposits within the earth. As a matter of fact, natural gas is sometimes found not too far away from crude oil deposits. Crude oil is the liquid fossil fuel, coal is the solid one, and natural gas is the gaseous fossil fuel.

People are sometimes confused by the term *natural gas* because they think (incorrectly) that it refers to the *gas* (gasoline) they use to fill their tanks. Although natural gas is sometimes used as a transportation fuel, the gasoline you buy at the gas station and natural gas have nothing to do with each other. The gasoline your car consumes is a product of crude oil, whereas natural gas is an entirely different member of the fossil fuel family, used primarily for heating, cooling, and cooking purposes.

Because of its importance as a source of energy, natural gas makes for a good investment. It's an important commodity with many applications. In this chapter, I present you with all the information you need to develop an investment strategy in the natural gas segment of energy. Because it's important to get all the facts up front about this commodity, I first provide you with hands-on information about the applicability of natural gas — how it's used and how you can profit from these uses. Then I give you a snapshot of the global natural gas market so you know who's producing it and who's consuming it. Identifying these patterns is a necessary part of developing a sound investment strategy. Finally, I show you how to actually start investing in and trading nat gas, as traders sometimes call it. Natural gas may not get the same kind of attention as crude oil, but it still makes for a great investment!

What's the Use? Looking at Natural Gas Applications

Because it's one of the cleanest-burning fossil fuels, natural gas has become increasingly popular as an energy source. In the United States alone, natural gas accounts for nearly a quarter of total energy consumption and is second only to petroleum when it comes to generating energy in the United States.

So who uses all this natural gas? The primary consumers of this commodity are the industrial sector, commercial interests, residential elements, transportation, and electricity generation. I list the consumption ratio of these sectors in Figure 4-1.

How do you measure natural gas?

Measuring natural gas can be confusing because multiple measurement methods exist. These measurements basically boil down to how much physical natural gas there is and how much energy the natural gas generates.

Whereas crude oil is measured in barrels (each barrel contains 42 gallons of oil), natural gas is measured in cubic feet. Recall from chemistry class that a cubic foot is a measure of volume for a square prism with six sides, each 1 foot in length. (The technical name for this shape is a *regular hexahedron,* but you can simply think of it as the shape of a sugar cube!) Because natural gas is in a gaseous state, it's easier to measure it in cubic feet. Sometimes natural gas is converted into liquid form, known as liquefied natural gas (LNG), which I cover in the section "Liquefied Natural Gas: Getting Liquid Without Getting Wet." LNG is also measured in cubic feet.

The abbreviation for cubic feet is *cf* (both letters are lower case). Therefore, 10 cubic feet is abbreviated as 10 cf. To have practical applications, cubic feet must be able to measure large amounts of volume. Consider the abbreviations for measuring larger volume amounts of cubic feet:

- 100 cubic feet: 1 Ccf
- 1,000 cubic feet: 1 Mcf
- 1 million cubic feet: 1 Mmcf
- 1 billion cubic feet: 1 Bcf
- 1 trillion cubic feet: 1 Tcf

Note that *cf* is always in lower case, and the first letter of the abbreviation is always capitalized. Many futures contracts based on natural gas are measured in cubic feet.

Natural gas can also be measured by the amount of energy it generates. This energy content is captured by a unit of measurement known as the *British thermal unit,* or *Btu.* One Btu measures the amount of heat necessary to increase the temperature of 1 pound of water by 1°F. To put it in perspective, 1 cf is the equivalent of 1,027 Btu. British thermal units, sometimes called *therms,* may appear on your gas bill to express the amount of natural gas your household consumed during a particular period of time.

For investment purposes, however, natural gas is generally quantified by using cubic feet.

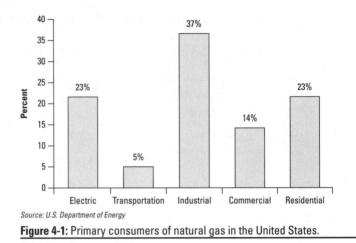

Source: U.S. Department of Energy

Figure 4-1: Primary consumers of natural gas in the United States.

Industrial uses of natural gas

The industrial sector is the largest consumer of natural gas, accounting for almost 40 percent of total consumption. Although industrial uses of natural gas have always played a major role in the sector, their significance has increased during the last several years and will continue to do so. As you can see in Figure 4-2, the industrial sector has always accounted for a large part of natural gas use, and because this trend will continue, it's a good area to consider investing in. (Actually, demand for natural gas products as a whole will increase throughout the first quarter of the 21st century, for reasons I discuss in the next section.)

Increased industrial demand should put upward price pressures on natural gas. One way to profit from this demand is by buying long natural gas futures.

As an investor, looking at long-term trends helps you develop an investment strategy that takes advantage of the market fundamentals.

So what specific parts of the industrial sector use natural gas? Natural gas is a truly versatile form of energy because it has many applications in industry. Consider a few industrial applications of natural gas products:

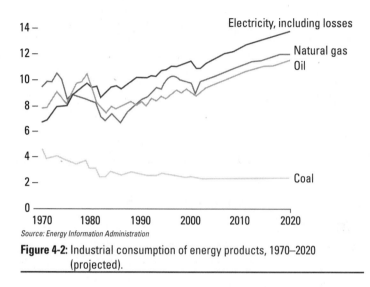

Source: Energy Information Administration

Figure 4-2: Industrial consumption of energy products, 1970–2020 (projected).

✔ Feedstock for fertilizers

✔ Food processing

✔ Glass melting

✔ Industrial boiler fueling

✔ Metal smelting

✔ Waste incineration

 The chemical composition of natural gas consists primarily of *methane,* a hydrocarbon molecule. It also includes other hydrocarbons, such as *butane, ethane,* and *propane* — all gases that have important industrial uses.

 When the industrial sector is firing on all cylinders, so to speak, demand for natural gas tends to increase. Keep an eye out for increased activity from the industrial sector because this is a bullish sign for natural gas. One indicator you can use to gauge the economic output from the industrial sector is the *Producer Price Index* (PPI). The PPI measures the average change in prices producers get for their products, expressed as a percent change. The PPI, compiled by the Bureau of Labor Statistics (BLS), is a good measure of the health in the industrial sector. You can get the latest PPI reports at www.bls.gov/ppi.

Natural gas in your home

Residential use accounts for almost a quarter of total natural gas consumption (refer to Figure 4-1). A large portion of homes in the United States, as well as other countries, use natural gas for both their cooking and heating needs — the two largest applications of natural gas in the home.

About 70 percent of households in the United States have natural gas ovens in the kitchen. The use of natural gas for cooking purposes has steadily increased as technological developments have allowed for an efficient and safe use of natural gas. How does this affect you as an investor? As long as folks need to cook, you can bet that natural gas will be there to fill this important need. This essential usage ensures that demand from the residential sector for natural gas will remain strong — a bullish sign for nat gas.

More than 50 percent of homes in the United States use natural gas for heating purposes. One way to benefit from this particular application is to identify peak periods of natural gas consumption. Specifically, demand for natural gas for heating increases in the Northern Hemisphere during the winter seasons. Therefore, one way to profit in the natural gas markets is to calibrate your strategy to this cyclical, weather-related trend. In other words, all things constant, natural gas prices should go up during the winters as folks seek to stay warm.

Although my aim in this book is to help you make money by *investing* in commodities such as natural gas, I'm going to take the liberty of showing you how to *save* money by using natural gas in your home. Natural gas is one of the cheapest energy forms, as measured by dollars per unit of energy generated. Look at Figure 4-3, and you'll quickly realize that you get more energy from natural gas per dollar (as measured in British thermal units, the standard energy measurement unit) than from almost any other source. Using natural gas may save you some money during the winters — which you can then use to bulk up your commodities investments!

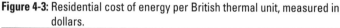

Source: U.S. Department of Energy

Figure 4-3: Residential cost of energy per British thermal unit, measured in dollars.

Natural gas's commercial uses

About 40 percent of the energy consumed by commercial users, such as hospitals and schools, comes from natural gas, accounting for about 15 percent of total natural gas consumption.

Because commercial users include establishments such as schools, hospitals, restaurants, movie theaters, malls, and office buildings, demand for natural gas from these key drivers of the economy rises during times of increasing economic activity. This trend means that, all things equal, you need to be bullish on natural gas during economic growth. (For more on gauging economic activity, see Chapter 2.)

One place to look for important economic clues that affect demand for natural gas is the Energy Information Administration (EIA), a division of the U.S. Department of Energy (DOE). The EIA provides a wealth of information regarding consumption trends of key energy products, such as natural gas, from various economic sectors. For information on the commercial usage of natural gas, visit www.eia. doe.gov/oiaf/aeo/aeoref_tab.html.

Generating electricity with natural gas

Natural gas is quickly becoming a popular alternative for generating electricity, with just less than 25 percent of natural gas usage going toward generating electricity. Actually, natural gas is used to produce approximately 10 percent of electricity generation in the United States. As you can see from Figure 4-4, that figure will increase dramatically in the coming years.

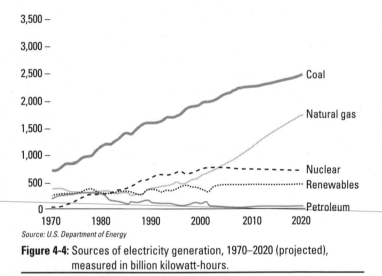

Source: U.S. Department of Energy

Figure 4-4: Sources of electricity generation, 1970–2020 (projected), measured in billion kilowatt-hours.

The long-term trend is that more natural gas will be required to generate electricity. This increased demand from a critical sector will keep upward pressures on natural gas prices over the long term. Keep this in mind as you consider investing in this commodity.

Natural gas and transportation

It's not a widely known fact, but natural gas is used in a number of vehicles (approximately three million worldwide) as a source of fuel. These vehicles, known simply as *natural gas vehicles* (NGV), run on a grade of natural gas called *compressed natural gas* (CNG). This usage accounts for only about 5 percent of total natural gas consumption, but demand for NGV may increase as a viable (cheaper) alternative to gasoline (a crude oil derivative).

Since the first edition of this book, NGVs have become much more prevalent. As of 2015, more than 15 million NGVs are in circulation worldwide. The most dominant countries using

NGVs are Pakistan, Argentina, Brazil, and Iran. Expect to see more of these vehicles on the road as countries continue their shift toward cleaner sources of transportation fuels.

Keep a close eye on technological developments of natural gas in the transportation sector. If natural gas grabbed a slice of the transportation market, which now accounts for almost two-thirds of crude oil consumption, prices for natural gas could increase dramatically. For the latest on NGV, consult the *International Association of Natural Gas Vehicles,* at www.iangv.org.

Liquefied Natural Gas: Getting Liquid Without Getting Wet

Liquefied natural gas, or LNG, is a recent development in the field. LNG is exactly what it says it is: natural gas in a liquid form. The reason for this development is quite simple: As demand for natural gas increases, you need to be able to transport this precious commodity across vast distances (for example, across continents and through oceans). Transporting it is difficult to do when it's in a gaseous state. Enter LNG, which is nothing but natural gas in a liquid state to make it easy to transport.

Transforming natural gas from its gaseous state into a liquid state is a complex process. The natural gas must first be cooled to a temperature of –260°F to transform it to its liquid state. An additional advantage of LNG is that it takes up considerably less space — about 600 times less — which means that you can transport a lot more of it farther and more economically. When the natural gas is in a liquid state, it's usually transported in specially designed tankers to consumer markets. (I present some of the companies that transport energy products around the world in Chapter 6.) Before it's actually delivered to consumers, it goes through a regasification process.

In the United States, most natural gas is transported through pipelines in a gaseous state. The natural gas pipeline system in the United States is one of the most extensive in the world — 300 million miles of pipeline — and it connects major natural gas–producing regions (such as the Gulf of Mexico) to large natural gas consumers (such as the East Coast). Although the pipeline remains the dominant method of transporting natural gas, LNG is quickly establishing itself as a viable source of natural gas, particularly as domestic production declines and imports increase. Some of the major operators of these pipelines that transport both natural gas and LNG are entities known as *master limited partnerships* (MLPs). The good news is that you can profit from moving natural gas across the United States by investing in MLPs, covered in Chapter 14.

In 2005, the United States received only about 1 percent of its total natural gas (170 Bcf) through LNG. By 2010, that figure had shifted dramatically upward, coming in at 452 Bcf. The top six exporters of LNG to the United States include Trinidad and Tobago, Egypt, Algeria, Nigeria, Norway, and Qatar. This trend is now well established and is set to increase in the coming years.

Investing in Natural Gas

The future for natural gas looks bright. The total natural gas consumption on a global scale in 2015 was approximately 125 trillion cubic feet (125 Tcf). In 2010, that figure increased to 120 Tcf. By 2020, that figure is estimated to increase by more than 20 percent, to 156 Tcf, as you can see in Figure 4-5.

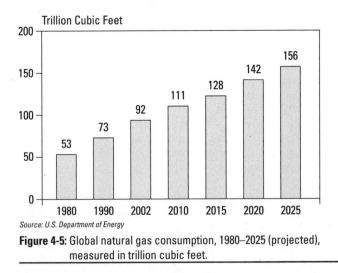

Source: U.S. Department of Energy

Figure 4-5: Global natural gas consumption, 1980–2025 (projected), measured in trillion cubic feet.

Knowing that demand for natural gas will remain steady until 2025 is an important piece of information for you as an investor. Perhaps even more important is figuring out which countries and companies will be meeting this demand. Determining who's going to be supplying this natural gas will help you devise an investment strategy to profit from this increased natural gas demand. Table 4-1 lists the countries with the largest reserves of natural gas in the world.

Table 4-1	Top Ten Natural Gas Reserves by Country, 2015		
Rank	*Country*	*Proven Reserves (Tcf)*	*Percent of World Total*
1	Russia	1,680	27.8%
2	Iran	1,050	15.9%
3	Qatar	910	15.1%
4	Saudi Arabia	235	3.9%
5	United Arab Emirates	212	3.5%
6	Nigeria	190	3.1%
7	United States	189	3.1%
8	Algeria	161	2.7%
9	Venezuela	151	2.5%
10	Iraq	110	1.8%

Global natural gas reserves are estimated at 6,040 Tcf, which is the equivalent of approximately 6 quadrillion cubic feet (quadrillion, not zillion, is the next figure above trillion). You can get exposure to this huge natural gas market in a couple ways: by trading futures contracts or by investing in companies that are involved in the production and development of natural gas fields in some of the countries listed in Table 4-1. I discuss the pros and cons of each investment method in the following sections.

Trading nat gas futures

The most direct method of investing in natural gas is to trade futures contracts on one of the designated commodities exchanges. The Chicago Mercantile Exchange (CME), the exchange for energy products, gives you the option to buy and sell natural gas futures and options.

To trade futures, you need to have a futures account with a designated broker, known as the *futures commission merchant* (FCM). After you open a futures account, you can start trading these derivative products. For more on futures and options, turn to Chapter 13.

The natural gas futures contract is the second-most popular energy contract on the CME, right behind crude oil. It's traded under the ticker symbol NG, and it trades in increments of 10,000 Mmbtu. You can trade it during all the calendar months, to periods up to 72 months after the current month. (I cover tradability in Chapter 12.)

The CME offers a mini version of this contract for individual hedgers and speculators. Check out the nat gas section of the CME Web site for more on this contract: www.cmegroup.com/trading/energy/natural-gas/natural-gas.html.

Trading natural gas futures contracts and options isn't for the fainthearted. Even by commodities standards, natural gas is a notoriously volatile commodity, subject to wild price fluctuations. If you're not an aggressive investor willing to withstand the financial equivalent of a wild roller-coaster ride, nat gas futures may not be for you. To give you a picture of the prices, Figure 4-6 shows a historical overview of the price action of the CME natural gas contract.

Nat gas companies: The natural choice

Investing in companies that process natural gas is a positive investment choice because it offers you exposure to this market through the expertise and experience of industry professionals, without the volatility of the futures market. Some natural gas companies are involved in the production of natural gas fields; others are responsible for delivering natural gas directly to consumers.

Figure 4-6: CME natural gas futures contract performance, 2001–2010 (dollars per thousand cubic feet).

I list companies that are *fully integrated* natural gas companies, which means they're involved in all the production, development, transportation, and distribution phases of natural gas. Investing in these companies gives you a solid foothold in this industry. Here's your hit list:

- ✔ **Allegheny Energy (NYSE: AYE):** Provides natural gas–based electricity to consumers in the eastern United States, primarily in Pennsylvania, Virginia, and Maryland. This S&P 500 company is a good option if you want regional exposure to natural gas production.

- ✔ **Alliant Energy (NYSE: LNT):** Provides consumers with natural gas and electricity derived from natural gas throughout the United States. This company is a good choice if you want exposure to the North American nat gas market.

- ✔ **Nicor Inc. (NYSE: GAS):** Nicor's operations are primarily centered in Illinois, where it provides natural gas to more than two million consumers. This company is another good regional investment.

For a complete listing of companies involved in natural gas production and distribution, look at the American Gas Association Web site: www.aga.org.

Chapter 5

Investing in Renewable and Alternative Energy

*T*wo problems plague traditional sources of energy, such as oil, natural gas, and coal: their increasing monetary cost and their increasing opposition from environmentalists concerned about the hazards of burning these fuels. It's not hard to see that renewable sources of energy, such as solar and wind power, will attract more attention in the near future. Since the first edition of this book was published, renewable energy as an industry has received a tremendous amount of media, social, and political coverage. The number of experts in this field has mushroomed, as has the number of companies involved. Many factors account for this increased attention, least of all the calls for countries to reduce their fossil fuel consumption in light of the global environmental impact of burning such fuels.

The field of renewable energy is getting a lot of attention, and there's certainly potential to make some money in this field. In this chapter, I give you an overview of this dynamic industry and focus on specific fields — including solar energy, wind power, and biofuels — to help you develop an investment strategy rooted in the market fundamentals. I also go through the global energy scene and identify some of the major trends affecting it. I show you how to profit from other segments of the energy market, such as coal, nuclear power, and electricity.

Getting to Know Renewable Energy

In practical terms, *renewable energy* refers to sources of energy that are essentially always present, always available, and always renewable. The sun and wind are traditional sources of renewable energy because the sun always shines and the wind always blows, day in and day out. Harnessing these renewable sources of energy is beneficial for a couple reasons. First, they're always there. Second, they don't emit any greenhouse gases, which decreases pollution output.

The benefits of renewable energy are obvious, but one of the big obstacles to implementing a large-scale, global industry is less obvious: cost. For instance, the cost of harnessing the power of the sun to generate electricity is extremely high and requires massive commitments of capital expenditures. The solar industry currently needs heavy government subsidies to be able to generate enough profits to remain competitive; the same applies to wind energy and other types of renewable energy, such as ethanol.

Renewable energy as a whole represents only a small fraction of the total energy landscape in the United States, which is also attributable to the broader global footprint. Getting exposure to some of these sectors from an individual portfolio perspective is difficult. For example, unless you own or operate geothermal plants, you have few direct methods for getting this kind of exposure. For this reason, I focus only on renewable energy sources for which there are tradable, liquid, and transparent instruments — specifically, solar, wind, and biomass.

Although it's currently more challenging to get direct exposure to different renewable energy submarkets (such as geothermal), this will undoubtedly change in the future as more instruments are made available and as the market gains more breadth and credibility. In addition, you can adopt a creative approach to getting this kind of exposure; for example, if you want to get exposure to hydroelectric power generation, you can examine the electric utilities universe for companies that have hydroelectric power assets. This strategy may not give you that direct investment route, but you can still manage to generate indirect exposure in your portfolio.

If you're interested in keeping up-to-date on the latest developments in the renewable energy space, I recommend that you check out the Department of Energy's Energy Efficiency and Renewable Energy (EERE) initiative, at www.eere.energy.gov. For the United Nations' official intergovernmental policy view on global warming and greenhouse gases, consult the Intergovernmental Panel on Climate Change (IPCC), at www.ipcc.ch.

Investing in solar energy

Solar power currently accounts for only 1 percent of total renewable energy sources, but it's one of the fastest-growing areas in the space. Governments around the world are in the process of announcing massive infrastructure spending programs dedicated to harnessing the sun's power and turning it into electricity and other forms of energy.

India and China have been at the forefront of this trend, with $30 billion in projects announced in the 20 years ahead. Even countries that you may not associate with renewable energy are taking the lead on this matter; Saudi Arabia, the world's largest oil producer, and the United Arab Emirates have both dedicated large budgets to the development of solar power. Even the Kingdom of Morocco has jumped on the bandwagon, with 3,000 megawatts projected by 2020 to come from solar plants located in the Sahara Desert.

Broadly speaking, solar power is the process by which energy from the sun is harnessed and channeled into a usable energy form, generally heat or electricity. Two different processes can transform solar power:

- ✔ **Solar photovoltaic energy:** Don't be intimidated by this high-sounding name — it simply describes the method by which energy from the sun is captured and transformed into electricity.

- ✔ **Solar thermal energy:** This method transforms the sun's energy into heat, which may be used for a number of different purposes, such as interior space heating or water heating. If you've ever seen flat-panel solar collectors mounted on homes or buildings, they're used for solar thermal energy purposes.

Many companies are trying to turn these two methods of transforming solar energy into a commercially viable enterprise, but they face some challenges. One of the biggest impediments to the commercial success of solar power is the sun itself! Specifically, the sun isn't a resource that you can control. For one thing, you can't manipulate the weather, so you're at the mercy of rain, fog, clouds, the earth's rotation, and other natural external factors that block the sun. For this reason, solar power accounted for around 0.56 percent of the electricity produced in the United States in 2015.

Currently, the equity markets give you a direct way to get exposure to the solar industry. Following are some of the top names in the industry to choose from:

- ✔ **First Solar, Inc. (NASDAQ: FSLR):** FSLR was one of the first solar companies to go public. It's involved in the manufacture and sales of photovoltaic solar panels to end users, including governments, corporate entities, and private individuals. Its two main revenue generators come from the components sector (selling parts for specific solar projects) and the systems segment (installation of solar farms). With net profit margins in excess of 22 percent (2010 figures), this company offers solid exposure to the photovoltaic market segment.

- ✔ **Suntech Power Holdings (NYSE: STP):** Suntech is a world leader in the development, design, and implementation of solar photovoltaic systems and products. In addition to providing construction services, the company offers engineering and maintenance services to its clients around the world. It has a global footprint, with operations in Germany, the United States, Australia, South Africa, Japan, and South Korea. For a truly diversified global exposure to the solar industry, be sure to consider Suntech.

Trading in wind energy

Wind energy is another renewable resource that's getting increasing attention from investors. Energy is generated by huge wind machines (similar to traditional windmills), which are placed side by side in *wind farms*.

The challenge to wind energy is that it's dependent on the wind, a very unpredictable natural phenomenon. Wind has traditionally held a small part in the energy generation spectrum, but it's increasing as it becomes a cost-effective solution. Currently, few publicly traded companies deal specifically in wind power.

That said, many industrial companies are beginning to implement large-scale investments in wind energy production. If you're looking for some indirect exposure to wind, you can always consider an investment in General Electric (NYSE: GE). Although GE is known for its large industrial footprint, it's becoming one of the leaders in the wind space and is the global leader in manufacturing and sales of wind turbines across dozens of markets.

With rising energy prices, wind energy may get more focus. If you're interested in investing in wind power and want to stay on top of emerging trends, check out the American Wind Energy Association, at www.awea.org. The site maintains a database of private companies involved in wind energy that may go public one day.

Betting on biomass

Biomass is currently the biggest component of the renewable energy industry, accounting for 53 percent of total production estimates. Scientifically speaking, biomass energy is produced by processing common wastes and transforming them into renewable energy through a biochemical conversion process.

Some common feedstock is used in this process:

- ✓ Corn
- ✓ Ethanol
- ✓ Eucalyptus
- ✓ Forestry crop residues
- ✓ Industrial residues
- ✓ Municipal solid wastes
- ✓ Palm oil
- ✓ Sugarcane
- ✓ Vegetable oil

As you can see, the raw material inputs are varied and come from a wide array of sources, which offers benefits and competitive advantages to the industry. Specifically, because such a large number of inputs are available, the process can be replicated across different markets, landscapes, and geographies. For example, agriculturally rich countries such as Brazil can process large amounts of agricultural wastes (such as ethanol and sugarcane waste) to generate energy; on the other hand, countries with large industrial apparatuses, such as Russia, can also take advantage of the biomass process by using industrial residues and municipal wastes as primary inputs. The process is thus versatile and scalable, which accounts for its ubiquity in the energy spectrum.

For now, investors have no direct plays into the biomass and biofuels market; in the current industry structure, only privately held companies, municipalities, and other governmental institutions run biomass plants and operations.

However, a company located in Brazil is a world leader in biomass generation: *CPFL Energia* (CPFL). CPFL generates, distributes, and sells electricity to the Brazilian domestic market. It derives a significant portion of its revenues from biomass generation, specifically the transformation of sugarcane waste into electricity. The company trades on the Sao Paulo Stock Exchange (the *BOVESPA*) but recently listed its shares on the New York Stock Exchange under the ticker CPL, via an American Depository Receipt (ADR).

 As a result, you can now get exposure to an exciting market that was nonexistent only a few years ago. I expect more companies involved in the biomass space to go public in the coming years, giving you a broader range of options to choose from. In the meantime, I encourage you to monitor CPFL.

Digging Up Further Energy Sources

As the global population increases and emerging countries industrialize, the demand for energy products will rise throughout the first quarter of the 21st century. The Energy Information Administration (EIA) anticipates that global demand for energy products will increase by more than 70 percent between 2003 and 2030.

In 2015, fossil fuels (oil, natural gas, and coal) accounted for 82 percent of total energy consumption. Crude oil alone was responsible for almost 40 percent of global energy use. However, as the price of these traditional energy sources increases (driven by both strong demand and limited supply), the calls for new sources of energy are increasing as well.

Despite numerous calls, however, the energy landscape is unlikely to change anytime soon, which means that fossil fuels will remain the dominant source of global energy for years to come. Alternative energies may generate a lot of attention, but how much actual progress will be made is still up in the air. Keep this in mind as you're looking at investing in these alternatives.

For example, take a look at Figure 5-1. You can see that the energy picture until 2030 will remain fairly static on a percentage basis; fossil fuels will continue to be the dominant fuel for the global economy, and alternatives will keep playing an important but less significant role.

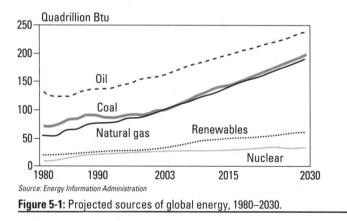

Source: Energy Information Administration

Figure 5-1: Projected sources of global energy, 1980–2030.

Despite the dominance of fossil fuels, particularly crude oil, the alternative space is a dynamic area and a fertile ground for investment opportunities.

Reexamining coal

In 2009 in the United States (the world's most important energy market), coal accounted for 23 percent of total fossil fuel consumption. Therefore, coal is still an important source of energy and can provide some good moneymaking opportunities.

Coal is used primarily for electricity generation (steam coal) and steel manufacturing (metallurgical coal). Besides its practical uses in these two important areas, coal is an increasingly popular fossil fuel because of its large reserves. Specifically, companies in the United States have long touted the benefits of moving toward a more coal-based economy because the United States has the largest coal reserves in the world.

Coal is measured in short tons. One *short ton* is the equivalent of 2,000 lbs. In terms of energy, one short ton of *anthracite,* the coal of highest quality, contains approximately 25 million Btu of energy.

Because the United States, Russia, and China collectively hold more than 55 percent of the world's total coal reserves, investing in a coal company with large operations in any of these countries gives you exposure to this important segment of the market.

Just because a country has large deposits of a natural resource, however, doesn't mean that it exploits them to full capacity. To give you a better idea of this market characteristic, I list in Table 5-1 the top coal-producing countries.

Table 5-1	Hard Coal Production by Country, 2015	
Rank	**Country**	**Production (Million Short Tons)**
1	China	2,971
2	United States	919
3	India	526
4	Australia	335
5	Indonesia	263

Rank	Country	Production (Million Short Tons)
6	South Africa	248
7	Russia	229
8	Kazakhstan	96
9	Poland	78
10	Colombia	73

Demand for coal is expected to increase during the first quarter of the 21st century, as you can see in Figure 5-2. Most of this growth will come from the emerging market economies, particularly the economies of China and India, which will account for approximately 75 percent of the demand increase for coal. (China is currently the largest consumer of coal in the world, ahead of the United States, India, and Japan.)

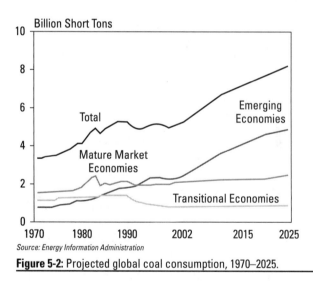

Source: Energy Information Administration

Figure 5-2: Projected global coal consumption, 1970–2025.

Demand for coal has resulted in strong price movements in the commodity itself. Before the 2008 Global Financial Crisis, prices for coal experienced a major uptrend, going from $50 per short ton in 2006 to almost $200 per short ton in 2008 (see Figure 5-3). The financial crisis resulted in a severe quasicrash scenario for coal prices, as was the case for several other important commodities. This correction was necessary

© John Wiley & Sons, Inc.

Figure 5-3: Spot price of coal in U.S. dollars per short ton, 2006–2010.

because the rally was overdone on the way up; coal prices seem to have stabilized in the $100 range, but expect much more activity surrounding this commodity in the future.

As with other fossil fuels, coal comes in different qualities. Specifically, coal comes in four categories, classified by its carbon, sulfur, and ash content, as well as by the level of energy it releases.

Here are the four major categories of coal:

- ✓ **Lignite:** Lignite contains the least amount of carbon and the most sulfur and ash of all coal types, so it's considered the least valuable. Sometimes called brown coal, it's primarily used in generating electricity.

- ✓ **Sub-bituminous:** This type of coal contains a little more carbon than lignite and thus is considered to be of a higher quality. It also has lower levels of sulfur and ash than lignite. It's used mostly to heat water in electricity-generating steam turbines.

- ✓ **Bituminous:** Because bituminous coal burns well and creates a lot of energy, it's of high value. The most common type of coal found in the United States, it's used to generate electricity and, in the steel industry, create high-quality steel.

✔ **Anthracite:** By far the most valuable type of coal, anthracite contains the highest levels of carbon and the least amount of sulfur and ash; it also provides the most energy on a per-unit basis. Because of its high value, anthracite is used for residential and commercial space heating.

Before you invest in companies involved in the coal business, find out which type of coal they produce. This information will help you better understand the company's business and profit margins. You can find this information in a company's annual and quarterly reports.

You can get access to the coal markets either by trading coal futures directly or by investing in coal companies.

Coal futures contract

As with other members of the fossil fuel family, coal has an underlying futures contract that trades on a commodity exchange — in this case, the Chicago Mercantile Exchange (CME). This coal contract gives commercial users (such as coal producers, electric companies, and steel manufacturers) the opportunity to hedge against market risk and offers speculators a chance to profit from this market risk. (For more on the CME and other commodity exchanges, turn to Chapter 14. Review Chapter 13 for more on futures contract specifications.)

The coal futures contract on the CME tracks the price of the *Central Appalachian* type of coal. Central Appalachian coal, known as CAPP, is a high-quality coal with low sulfur and ash content. The CAPP futures contract (which traders sometimes affectionately call "the big sandy" because it's produced in the area between West Virginia and Kentucky where the Ohio River flows) is the premium benchmark for coal prices in the United States.

The contract trades under the ticker symbol QL and is tradable during all the calendar months of the current year, in addition to all calendar months in the subsequent three years. Additional information on this futures contract is available on the CME Web site, at www.cmegroup.com.

Although the coal futures contract does offer you exposure to coal, be warned that the market for this contract is fairly illiquid, meaning that the trading volume is low. Most of the traders involved in this market represent large commercial interests that transact with each other. A few speculators trade the coal futures markets, but they don't represent a significant portion of the market. You may not be able to get involved directly in this market without large capital reserves to compete with the commercial interests.

Coal company

One of the best ways to invest in coal is to invest in a company that mines it. The following three companies are the best, in my opinion:

- ✔ **Arch Coal (NYSE: ACI):** Arch Coal is smaller in size than its main competitors, Peabody and Consol, but I like it because the coal it produces is of very high quality. It operates more than 30 mines in the continental U.S. and controls more than 3 billion short tons of reserves. It has operations in the largest coal-producing regions in the United States, including in the Appalachians, the Powder River Basin (on the Montana/Wyoming border), and the Western Bituminous region (on the Colorado/Utah border).

- ✔ **Consol Energy (NYSE: CNX):** With headquarters in Pittsburgh, Consol Energy has significant operations in the coal mines of Pennsylvania and nearby coal-rich states of West Virginia and Kentucky. As of 2009, it controlled 8 billion short tons of coal reserves, with operations in more than 17 mines across the United States. CNX is well positioned to take advantage of the booming domestic coal market.

- ✔ **Peabody Energy (NYSE: BTU):** Peabody Energy is the largest coal company, with approximately 15 billion short tons of coal reserves. The coal it produces is responsible for generating approximately 10 percent of the electricity in the United States. Peabody Energy is the largest coal company out there today; it's the ExxonMobil of coal companies. I like the company because of its size and because it has mining operations in the United States but also in Australia and Venezuela, two important coal markets. You can examine the price performance of this stock in Figure 5-4.

© John Wiley & Sons, Inc.

Figure 5-4: Equity performance of Peabody Energy, 2006–2010.

If you want to invest in coal companies with more international exposure to markets in Russia, China, and other coal-rich countries, I recommend that you consult the World Coal Institute, at www.worldcoal.org.

Investing in nuclear power

When most people think of nuclear power, they tend to think of nuclear weapons and mushroom clouds. However, nuclear power has an important civilian role, too. Civilian and commercial nuclear power is an integral part of the global energy supply chain and is a valuable energy source for residential, commercial, and industrial consumers worldwide. In fact, nuclear power generates more than 20 percent of the electricity in the United States. In countries like France, nuclear power generates more than 75 percent of electricity!

Nuclear power currently accounts for about 5 percent of total global energy consumption, and it's expected to remain at these stable levels until 2030. But if the price of fossil fuels rises (oil, natural gas, and coal) dramatically enough to start affecting demand (creating what is called *demand destruction*), nuclear power may play an important role in picking up the slack.

One way you can profit from increased interest in nuclear power is to invest in uranium, the most widely used fuel in nuclear power plants. However, you're not likely to hear about this opportunity from your local financial media because uranium is a pretty obscure investment area. But sometimes as an investor, you need to be able to think creatively and look at opportunities that other investors haven't considered. Investing in uranium to benefit from the increased demand in nuclear power is not a well-known or well-advertised investment play, but it can be profitable nevertheless.

You may be surprised to find that the period of 2000–2008 saw a major bull market in uranium, with prices moving from $20 per pound to almost $140 per pound. The Global Financial Crisis brought some sense back into the market, as this commodity attracted many players of a speculative nature (see Figure 5-5). Prices post-2008 went back to above precrisis levels, to a more reasonable $50 per pound, and this presents a potential opportunity for the discriminating investor.

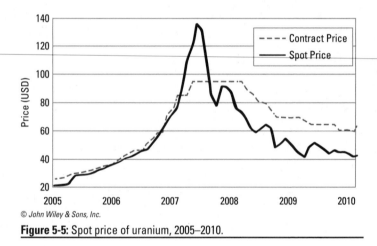

© John Wiley & Sons, Inc.

Figure 5-5: Spot price of uranium, 2005–2010.

Uranium equities

Because uranium isn't a widely tradable commodity, the best way to profit from this trend is to invest in companies that specialize in the mining, processing, and distribution of uranium for civilian nuclear purposes. I like these companies in this sector:

✔ **Cameco Corporation (NYSE: CCJ):** Cameco is the marquee name in the uranium mining space. The company operates four uranium mines in the United States and Canada. The company mines uranium and is also involved in refining and converting the uranium into fuel that's sold to nuclear power plants to generate electricity (see Figure 5-6).

© *John Wiley & Sons, Inc.*

Figure 5-6: Equity performance of Cameco Corporation, 2006–2010.

✓ **Strathmore Corporation (Toronto: STM):** Whereas UEX is involved in the exploration of uranium ore, Strathmore — another Canadian company — specializes in the mining of uranium. The company, which trades on the Toronto Stock Exchange, operates in the Athabasca region in Canada, as well as in the U.S.

✓ **UEX Corporation (Toronto: UEX):** UEX is a Canada-based mining company that specializes in the exploration and mining of uranium in the Athabasca basin. The Athabasca basin in Canada is an important region in global uranium mining that accounts for about 30 percent of total world production. The company is currently still in exploration phases, but it could become a real moneymaker if it comes across large deposits of uranium. The company trades on the Toronto Stock Exchange.

Uranium ETF

In addition to getting direct equity exposure, you can invest in uranium companies with the convenience of an exchange-traded fund (ETF). In 2010, ETF provider Global X Funds out of New York launched the first-ever uranium-based ETF, the Global X Uranium ETF (NYSE: URA).

URA tracks a basket of the most actively traded uranium stocks, as measured by the Solactive Global Uranium Index, its underlying benchmark. As such, URA gives you exposure to some of the most high-profile names in the industry, including Cameco, Uranium One, Paladin Resources, Denison Mines, and Kalahari Minerals. If you're looking for broad-based exposure to the uranium equity markets, URA is a good choice for your investment objectives. For more information on URA, visit www.globalxfunds.com. Chapter 12 tells you how you can incorporate ETFs into your trading strategy.

Uranium futures

If you have a good grip on futures trading and are looking for a new instrument to add to your portfolio, I'm happy to report that you can now invest directly in uranium itself. The Chicago Mercantile Exchange (CME) now offers the UxC (CME: UX), the first contract of its kind that gives you direct exposure to this precious resource. For more information on this contract, visit www.cmegroup.com.

Trading futures contracts involves a higher degree of risk due to the use of margin, volatility, and other factors. Make sure you trade futures contracts only if you already have plenty of experience. For more on trading these instruments, turn to Chapter 13.

For more information on nuclear power, the Energy Information Administration (EIA) has an excellent Web site with all sorts of practical information on this industry, at www.eia.doe.gov/fuelnuclear.html. The Ux Consulting Company is a great resource for everything regarding uranium and nuclear power. Its Web site is located at www.uxc.com.

Trading electricity

Have you ever wondered where the electricity that allows you to watch TV, use your air conditioner, or power your computer comes from? Getting electricity to residential, commercial, and industrial consumers is a lengthy process. The electricity is first created in a generator at a power plant and is then sent through transmission lines at very high voltages to a substation near consumers. The substation is equipped with a generator that transforms the high-voltage electricity into a low-voltage form, which is then sent to consumers via distribution lines. So how can you profit from it? It's quite simple.

Most of the electricity in the United States is generated through steam turbines. The water used to generate steam is heated to very high temperatures using traditional energy sources such as coal, natural gas, and nuclear power, as well as other renewable sources (such as wind and solar). Look at Figure 5-7 for a breakdown of how electricity is generated in the United States.

© *John Wiley & Sons, Inc.*

Figure 5-7: U.S. production of electricity by energy source, 2008.

Electricity is measured in watts, with 1 kilowatt equal to 1,000 watts and a megawatt equal to 1 million watts. In the power industry, watts are expressed in terms of hours of operation, where 1 kilowatt-hour (1 kWh) is 1,000 watts working for a period of 1 hour. Your electricity bill is measured in kilowatt-hours, and 1 kWh is the equivalent of 3,412 Btu. To put it in perspective, the United States consumed a grand total of 3,669 billion kWh of electricity in 2003.

As you can see from Figure 5-7, investing in coal as well as nuclear power is one way to invest in electricity. But you can invest directly in the power industry in several other ways as well.

Charged and ready to go

The most direct way of investing in electricity is . . . to buy it! The Chicago Mercantile Exchange (CME) offers a futures contract that tracks the price of electricity as administered by PJM Interconnection. PJM is a Regional Transmission Organization (RTO) that oversees the largest electric grid system in the world and services more than 50 million customers in the United States. It's responsible for generating more than 700 million megawatt-hours of electricity across 55,000 miles of transmission lines. Because of its dominance in the U.S. electricity market, the PJM electricity futures contract on the CME/NYMEX provides you with a widely recognizable and tradable electricity benchmark.

The PJM contract gives you the option of trading both *on-peak* and *off-peak* electricity hours. On-peak times are defined as Monday through Friday between 7 a.m. and 11 p.m., the times when the most electricity is consumed in the United States. Off-peak hours go from midnight to 7 a.m. local time Monday through Friday and include Saturday and Sunday as well. On-peak hours are usually more liquid because that's when most of the electricity is consumed.

The PJM contract is traded in units of 40 mWh (megawatt-hours) under the ticker symbol JM. For more information on this specific contract, check out the CME/NYMEX Web site, www.nymex.com/jm_desc.aspx. To find out more about futures contracts in general, turn to Chapter 13.

Although most of the market participants in the electricity futures market are local and regional power providers and suppliers, the futures contract lends itself to being traded by individual speculators as well. In recent years, as interest in commodities as an asset class has increased, the number of speculative participants in the electricity market has grown as well.

Power to the people

You probably get a letter from them every month, but you may have never given too much thought about the investment opportunities they present. I'm talking, of course, about electric utilities. *Utilities* are the companies responsible for providing electricity to millions of folks in the United States and around the world.

I like utilities for a number of reasons, particularly for their very high dividend payout. The industry has an average 5 percent dividend yield, one of the highest of any industry. However, remember when you're investing for dividend income that dividends are subject to market fluctuations. Table 5-2 lists some utilities to consider, along with their dividend yield.

Table 5-2	Publicly Traded Utilities, 2010 Dividend Yields	
Utility	**Ticker**	**Dividend Yield**
Great Plains Energy	NYSE: GXP	4.60%
Consolidated Edison	NYSE: ED	4.80%
Duke Energy Corp.	NYSE: DUK	5.50%
Dominion Resources	NYSE: D	4.30%
PG&E Corp.	NYSE: PCG	3.80%
Entergy Corp.	NYSE: ETR	4.70%

Dividends are a taxable source of income. Because of recent tax relief legislation, taxes on income generated through dividends are capped at 15 percent. However, Congress could always increase in the dividends tax rate. Keep a close eye on these dividend tax issues, because they'll have a direct impact on your utility investments.

In addition to juicy dividend yields, utilities offer you solid capital appreciation opportunities. Consider these companies when implementing your utility trading strategy.

✔ **Consolidated Edison (NYSE: ED):** If you live or have ever lived in New York, you're familiar with ConEd. ConEd is the main utility for New York State and New York City; its main line of business is regulated electric, gas, and steam delivery to wholesale and retail customers. ED provides electricity to more than 3.5 million clients and has a coverage of more than 650 square miles. This company is a good option if you're looking for exposure to the robust East Coast (especially New York) utility market.

✔ **Duke Energy Corp. (NYSE: DUK):** Duke Energy is one of the main players in the U.S. utility market. With a staggering 35,000 MW electricity-generating capacity, it has a footprint that spans the East Coast and the Midwest, and it has a portfolio in Latin America as well. In addition, Duke Energy owns and operates a natural gas–distribution business in Ohio and Kentucky, with an additional portfolio of renewable energy assets. With net profit margins of 14 percent (2015 figures), I recommend this company for broad-based utility exposure in the Americas.

Chapter 6

Totally Energized: Investing in Energy Companies

*O*ne way to play the energy markets is to invest in the companies involved in the production, transformation, and distribution of the world's most important energy commodities. In this chapter, I look at specialized energy and oil companies that are critical links in the global crude oil supply chain. This chain is long and convoluted, and these industries move in cycles, so identifying who does what allows you to develop a targeted investment strategy.

I show you in the following sections how to profit from the first step of the oil industry (exploration and production), through the transformational process (refining), and finally through the delivery system (transportation). Each of the companies operating in these segments of the market offers unique moneymaking investment opportunities. (See Chapter 3 for the goods on the large integrated oil companies — often referred to as "the majors" — that allow you to buy the market, so to speak, because they're involved in all facets of the global energy industry.)

Bull's-Eye! Profiting from Oil Exploration and Production

The oil industry starts in one place: at the oil field. The birth of the modern oil industry began with "Colonel" Edwin Drake's discovery of the first commercially viable oil field in Titusville, Pennsylvania, in 1859. (Drake wasn't really a colonel. He simply called himself that in order to get permits from the local authorities to drill for oil!) Ever since that day, individuals, companies, and countries have relentlessly pursued the discovery of oil fields and oil wells.

Among industry insiders, exploring for oil and gas is affectionately called *wildcatting.* Most wildcatting expeditions end up without any oil discoveries. When wildcatters drill a hole in the ground and no oil comes out, it's known as a *dry hole,* the unfortunate opposite of a *gusher,* a well that literally gushes oil.

The exploration and discovery of oil is a lucrative segment in the oil business. So how you can you strike it rich by discovering oil? Fortunately, you don't have to roll up your sleeves and go prospecting for oil in the Texas heartland. You can invest in companies that specialize in the exploration and production of oil fields, known in the business as *E&P.*

Oil wells are found in two places: on land and at sea. In recent years, offshore drilling has generated a lot of interest among investors, and a flurry of activity has been taking place in this sector as oil on land becomes scarcer. In this section, I introduce you to some of the companies involved in this exciting segment of the market.

Going offshore

The offshore drilling business is a technology-heavy industry, and you want to be familiar with some of the associated terminology, to make the most out of your investments.

Because offshore drilling activity may take place in unforgiving locations, companies have to deploy specific vessels for specific drilling projects. These vessels are among the most technologically advanced structures created by man. Some vessels are designed to withstand harsh winds and high waves. Others are more suited for shallow-water exploratory projects and need to move from location to location quickly.

You can get information on an offshore drilling company's fleet in its annual report. Companies usually lease these vessels to customers, which may include independent oil and gas companies, national oil companies, and the major integrated oil companies, for a premium. A company also includes this type of financial information regarding its fleet in the annual report.

Some of the leading companies in the offshore drilling business include the following:

- ✓ **Diamond Offshore Drilling (NYSE: DO):** With 50 offshore rigs, Diamond Offshore is one of the dominant players in the offshore drilling industry. Headquartered in Houston, Texas, DO has a wide global footprint, with deepwater drilling operations in Brazil, Scotland, Australia, and the Gulf of Mexico. The company has particular expertise in ultra deepwater drilling, with significant operations in Brazil through Petrobras, the state-owned oil company.

  As easily accessible oil becomes scarcer, I expect national oil companies and the majors to make more use of DO's deepwater expertise.

- ✓ **Noble Corporation (NYSE: NE):** Founded in 1921 in Texas, Noble is one of the oldest drilling contractors in the world. It has a fleet of more than 60 vessels and operations stretching from Brazil to the North Sea, and it has an edge in implementing technologically oriented solutions to meet customer demands.

  Noble Corporation has a subsidiary, Noble Technology Services Division, that's a sort of technological think tank dedicated to generating technical solutions for customers.

- ✓ **Transocean Inc. (NYSE: RIG):** Transocean, whose company motto is "We're never out of our depth," is the ExxonMobil of the offshore drillers. It's the largest company in terms of market capitalization and the size and scope of its operations. The company has more than 90 offshore drilling units at its disposal and is an expert in operating under harsh and extreme weather conditions. It has offshore operations in the U.S. Gulf of Mexico, Brazil, South Africa, the Mediterranean Sea, the North Sea, Australia, and Southeast Asia. In 2007, Transocean agreed to merge its operations with the operations of

GlobalSanteFe, the second-largest offshore driller at the time. The combined entity saw the addition of 60 vessels and an expanded global footprint, to include the Middle East and Canada. If you're looking for the largest and most diversified company in the group, Transocean is it.

If you want to dig deeper into this sector, you can check out the Web site www.rigzone.com, which includes up-to-date information on the offshore industry and the oil industry as a whole.

Staying on dry land

A large part of E&P activity takes place on dry land. Actually, the first commercially viable oil wells were discovered on land. Most industry insiders agree that most onshore oil wells have been discovered, but you can still benefit by investing in companies that are involved in the exploitation and production of onshore oil fields.

You may consider investing in a couple companies in this segment of the *drilling* market:

- ✔ **Nabors Industries (NYSE: NBR):** Nabors is one of the largest land-drilling contractors in the world. It has a division that can perform heavy-duty and horizontal drilling activities.

- ✔ **Patterson-UTI Energy Inc. (NASDAQ: PTEN):** Patterson-UTI is an onshore oil field drilling contractor that has extensive operations in North America. It operates in a number of segments, including drilling new wells and servicing and maintaining existing oil wells. It's part of the *S&P 400 MidCap* stocks.

Servicing the oil fields

Another area I recommend taking a close look at is companies that focus on oil field maintenance and services. The oil field services sector is dominated by technology-oriented and labor-intensive companies that seek to maximize an oil field's output by using sophisticated technological techniques, such as horizontal drilling and 3-D mapping and imaging.

The major integrated oil companies or national oil companies generally hire oil field services companies for general oil field and oil well maintenance and extraction solutions. For example, Saudi Aramco, the largest oil company in the world in terms of proven reserves, may turn to an oil field services company for the maintenance of a particular oil field. The services company may get involved in actually extracting crude from the oil well, providing data and statistics on current and past usage and on potential future output, using technologically oriented techniques to extract hard-to-recover oil, and performing other specific and general oil field–management services.

The added value of the oil field services companies is that they can improve oil recovery rates on existing fields and recover previously untapped oil pockets in old fields. As fewer oil fields are discovered, the world's major oil companies are looking for ways to maximize existing oil fields. Therefore, the role of the oil field services companies will become increasingly important in the future.

Perhaps the most well-known oil field services company is Halliburton (NYSE: HAL). A lot of people are familiar with the name because it's a high-profile Defense Department contractor that Vice President Dick Cheney once headed. Because of the nature of its political contracts, Halliburton is often a lightning rod for criticism. I recommend going beyond some of this criticism and directly analyzing the company's balance sheet, income statement, and other metrics to get a more accurate sense of the company's scope of operations. Although some of its work is political in nature (government contracts), that work represents only a fraction of its operational activities. More important, although Halliburton is the most notorious of the oil field services companies, it's certainly not representative of the other companies in the field. Many of the other players in this space focus exclusively on oil field maintenance and services, and aren't involved in work of a political nature.

These companies make up your hit list, if you're looking to invest in the oil field services space:

✔ **Baker Hughes, Inc. (NYSE: BHI):** As with most oil field services companies, Baker Hughes is headquartered in Houston, Texas. The company operates both in the United States and internationally, with operations stretching from the Persian Gulf to West Africa. Baker Hughes provides technologically oriented solutions to its customers to maximize oil field output efficiency. Baker Hughes isn't the biggest company in the group, but it's certainly a nimble competitor.

✔ **Halliburton Co. (NYSE: HAL):** This company, based in Houston, Texas, makes a lot of headlines (sometimes not very positive ones) because of the political nature of its work with the U.S. government and military. Besides its governmental contracts — which make up only a fraction of its revenues — the company is a leader in oil and gas field maintenance. It helps customers extract as much energy from existing wells as possible, while maintaining low costs. This makes Halliburton a knowledgeable company in the petroleum services sector.

✔ **Schlumberger Ltd. (NYSE: SLB):** Schlumberger may not be a household name, but it's well known and well regarded in the oil industry. The company is one of the most technologically savvy services companies out there and can provide solutions regarding all aspects of oil field–management services, from exploration and extraction to maintenance and abandonment. It provides evaluations to help customers identify the short-term and long-term viability of an oil field and specializes in maximizing oil field output through technologically advanced solutions.

For more information on the oil field services sector and all the companies involved in it, I recommend checking out the Yahoo! Finance Web site, at `biz.yahoo.com/ic/124.html`.

Oh My, You're So Refined! Investing in Refineries

Crude oil by itself doesn't have many useful applications — it needs to be refined into consumable products such as gasoline and jet fuel. Refineries are a critical link in the crude oil supply chain because, after crude oil is discovered, that oil needs to be transformed into products before it's sent to consumers.

This list details some of the products refineries derive from refining crude oil:

- ✓ Asphalt
- ✓ Automotive lubricating oil
- ✓ Diesel fuel
- ✓ Gasoline
- ✓ Heating oil (commercial and residential)
- ✓ Jet fuel (military and commercial aviation)
- ✓ Kerosene
- ✓ Petrochemicals
- ✓ Propane

Given the importance of these derivative products, you can imagine that you can make a lot of money investing in refineries. But before I give you a few company options, you need to look at three criteria when considering investing in companies that operate refineries:

- ✓ **Refinery throughput:** The capacity for refining crude oil over a given period of time, usually expressed in barrels
- ✓ **Refinery production:** Actual production of crude oil products, such as gasoline and heating oil
- ✓ **Refinery utilization:** The difference between production capacity, the throughput, and what's actually produced

You can find this information in a company's annual or quarterly reports.

The largest refinery in the United States is located in Baytown, Texas, and is operated by ExxonMobil. It has a refining capacity of 557,000 barrels per day. Most major integrated oil companies have a large refining capacity. These include some of the majors, like ExxonMobil and BP. One way to get exposure to the refining space is to invest in these major companies.

Another, more direct, way to profit from refining activity is to invest in independent refineries. The marquee name in this area is a company called The Valero Energy Corporation

(NYSE: VLO). Valero is the largest independent refining company in North America. It has a throughput capacity of 3.3 million barrels per day and operates the largest number of refineries in North America.

I like Valero because, if you want to play the refinery card, it gives you one of the most direct ways to do so. The major integrated companies are a good play, but they're so big that you don't get the same kind of direct exposure you do from Valero.

Although Valero is the goliath in the refinery space, a number of smaller companies can offer you a lot of value. Take a look at a couple of these companies:

- ✔ **Sunoco Inc. (NYSE: SUN):** Sunoco is the second-largest refiner in terms of total refinery throughput. It refines approximately 1 million barrels of crude oil a day into refined products, which it distributes primarily in the eastern United States.

  Sunoco, with headquarters in Philadelphia, operates refineries in Pennsylvania, Ohio, and New Jersey, and has a wide distribution network across the East Coast.

- ✔ **Tesoro Corp. (NYSE: TSO):** Tesoro, headquartered in San Antonio, Texas, is one of the leading refiners in the midcontinental and western United States. Its refineries transform crude oil into gasoline that's distributed through a network of about 500 retail outlets in the western United States. This option is a good regional play.

  It operates refineries in Utah, California, Washington, Alaska, and even Hawaii.

Refiners operate in an extremely cyclical industry, which poses an inherent investment risk that favors only the most savvy operators. An additional risk involves the very business model that refiners rely on. Independent refiners must purchase the raw material — crude oil — at market prices and must resell the finished product — gasoline, heating oil, and so on — at market prices. However, many majors also operate internal refineries that compete aggressively with the independents; whereas the independents must purchase the raw material at market prices, however, internal refineries often get oil at subsidized prices. This market dynamic makes it extremely difficult for independents to compete on an equal footing with the majors. Keep this in mind as you're analyzing independent refiners.

The Energy Information Administration compiles data on all U.S. refineries at www.eia.doe.gov/neic/rankings/refineries.htm.

Becoming an Oil Shipping Magnate

Commodities such as oil and gas would be useless if there was no way of transporting them to consumers. In fact, transporting commodities to consumers is probably as important as finding and processing them in the first place. Fortunately, as an investor, this need provides you with fertile ground to make money in the transportation of commodities.

This statistic can put things in perspective for you: Two out of every three barrels of oil that are transported are moved around in ships. The remaining one-third is transported via pipelines. (For more on how to invest in pipeline infrastructure, consider master limited partnerships, which I discuss in Chapter 14.) Therefore, the shipping industry plays a crucial role in the integrated oil business.

Perhaps no one person embodies the shipping industry like Aristotle Onassis, the Greek shipping magnate. Onassis built one of the largest fortunes in the world by shipping oil and other commodities around the world. Although I don't promise to make you as rich as Onassis, I'm confident that investing in the seaborne transportation business can give your portfolio a big boost.

In this section, I give you tools to help you invest in the oil-shipping business. I introduce you to the types of vessels that make up a modern oil tanker fleet, point out some of the major companies involved in the business, and offer you advice on pinpointing the right entry and exit points.

Transportation supply and demand

One of the most common questions I get asked about the oil-shipping industry is the following: What's the relationship between the price of crude oil and oil tanker profit margins? As with many good questions, this one has no straight answer. It depends on a lot of factors.

Tanker spot rates — the bread and butter of the shipping industry — are determined by supply and demand. The supply side, in this case, consists of how many ships are available to transport crude and products to the desired destinations around the world. On the demand side is how much crude oil and products need to be shipped from point A to point B. In the global shipping business, these factors are the two you need to watch closely.

For example, recently tanker spot rates have experienced some supply-side pressure. Because of a series of environmental incidents, in 1997 the International Maritime Organization (the global regulatory body of the shipping industry; www.imo.org) ordered the phasing out of all single-hull ships, to help prevent further oil spills.

Single-hull ships have just one layer of protection. *Double-hull ships* provide more protection against oil leaks because they have two layers, one exterior and one interior.

Shipping companies are planning to replace these single-hull ships with double-hull ships, but as with almost anything that has to do with the commodities business, constructing these ships takes time. Therefore, the supply-side pressure on tanker spot rates will remain until these newly designed double-hull ships are brought onboard. On the demand side of the equation, demand for crude oil and products worldwide remains robust.

Another important demand factor that many industry onlookers sometimes overlook is *oil import dependency.* Crude oil demand is critical, but if oil could be produced and consumed without the need to transport it across long distances on seaborne voyages, the oil-shipping industry would be out of business. The lifeblood of the global oil tanker business is the international flow of oil across countries and continents, or the dependence on oil imports. One key metric to help you gauge the level of activity in this area is global import and export data, which the Energy Information Administration's energy statistics division monitors. Its Web site is `www.eia.doe.gov/oil_gas/petroleum/info_glance/petroleum.html`.

As long as the supply of ships remains tight and the demand for crude oil seaborne transportation remains high, tanker spot rates will stay elevated. Now, to the extent that crude oil prices affect the demand of crude oil worldwide, crude oil prices will have an effect on tanker spot rates. Specifically, if crude oil prices go so high that folks are no longer willing to buy crude, thus causing demand destruction, the demand for shipping crude oil worldwide will also decrease, causing tanker spot rates to go down as well. However, this rate drop is an indirect effect of rising oil prices, which is why the relationship between crude oil prices and tanker spot rates isn't easily quantifiable. Too many variables are at play.

At the end of the day, as long as there's a demand for crude to be transported from producers to consumers, you can rest assured that oil shippers will remain in business.

Crude oil ships ahoy!

One factor you need to consider as you're planning investments in the oil-shipping industry is the ships themselves. Before you invest in a tanker stock, closely examine the fleet of vessels it operates.

Besides their catchy names, these vessels are identified by how much crude oil and products they can transport on sea. The unit of measurement used to capture this capacity is known as the *Dead Weight Ton,* or DWT. DWT measures the weight of the vessel, including all cargo it's carrying. Most ships are constructed in such a way that 1 DWT is the equivalent of 6.7 barrels of oil.

Table 6-1 lists the DWT capacity of the vessels described previously, along with their equivalent in barrels of oil.

Table 6-1 Vessel Capacity in DWT and Oil Equivalents

Vessel Type	Dead Weight Tons	Oil Equivalent (Barrels)
ULCC	320,000 and up	2+ million
VLCC	200,000–320,000	2 million
Suezmax	120,000–200,000	1 million
Aframax	80,000–120,000	600,000
Panamax	50,000–80,000	300,000

Masters of the sea: Petroleum shipping companies

The companies responsible for transporting crude oil and petroleum products are an essential link in the global energy supply chain. This group is a diverse bunch, and each company provides a necessary and important service to this crucial industry. Some companies concentrate their operations regionally, such as in the Gulf of Mexico or the Persian Gulf. Others have extensive transportation capabilities with operations in all four corners of the globe. Some operate a small group of VLCC vessels, whereas others operate a large number of smaller vessels. Still others specialize in shipping only crude oil, and others focus primarily on petroleum products such as gasoline.

With so many options to choose from, trying to identify which company to invest in can be confusing. In this section, I list all the major publicly traded oil-shipping companies, and I go through their operations and scope of activities so you can decide which one is right for your investment needs.

✔ **Frontline Ltd. (NYSE: FRO):** Founded in 1948, Frontline is one of the oldest shipping companies in the world. It also operates one of the world's largest fleets of VLCC vessels, with more than 44 VLCCs. Frontline also owns more than 35 Suezmax vessels (1 million barrel capacity), making it one of the largest tanker companies in the world in terms of transportation capacity. Cumulatively, Frontline has the capacity of 18 million DWT. With operations in the Persian Gulf, Europe, the United States, and Asia, Frontline runs a very tight ship indeed!

In addition to its tanker fleet, Frontline offers shareholders one of the highest dividend payouts I've ever seen: an eye-popping $6 per share. At current market prices, that's a yield of more than 18 percent! (See Table 6-2 for more on dividend yields.)

✔ **General Maritime Corp. (NYSE: GMR):** General Maritime focuses on the small and midsize segment of the tanker market. It operates a fleet of Suezmax and Aframax vessels, with operations primarily focused in the Atlantic basin. General Maritime links producers and consumers from Western Africa, the North Sea, the Caribbean, the United States, and Europe. If you're looking for exposure to the trans-Atlantic oil seaborne trade, GMR is a good bet.

The fact that GMR offers a $5 dividend per share also makes this an attractive tanker stock.

✔ **Overseas Shipholding Group, Inc. (NYSE: OSG):** Unlike many of its competitors, which are incorporated in offshore locations such as Bermuda and the Bahamas, OSG is headquartered in New York City. Although it has an international presence, it's the only company with a large presence in the American shipping market. Its U.S. vessels are mainly engaged in transporting crude oil from Alaska to the continental United States, and products from the Gulf of Mexico to the East Coast.

Additionally, OSG has one of the highest profit margins in the industry. If you're interested in the domestic crude oil transportation market, take the plunge with OSG.

✔ **Teekay Shipping Corp. (NYSE: TK):** Teekay Shipping is one of the world's largest seaborne transporters of crude oil and crude oil products. It operates a fleet of more than 130 vessels, including one VLCC (2 million barrel capacity) that transports crude from the Persian Gulf and West Africa to Europe, the United States, and Asia; about 15 Suezmax vessels (1 million barrel capacity) that connect producers in North Africa (Algeria) and West Africa to consumers in Europe and the United States; and more than 40 Aframax vessels (0.6 million barrel capacity) that operate in the North Sea, the Black Sea, the Mediterranean Sea, and the Caribbean.

In addition to conventional tankers, Teekay operates a fleet of offshore tankers that are constructed to transport crude from offshore locations to onshore facilities. If you're interested in a truly global and diversified oil-shipping company, you can't go wrong with Teekay Shipping.

Table 6-2   Oil Tanker Stocks, 2010 Dividend Yields

Company	Ticker	Dividend Yield
Frontline	NYSE: FRO	10.9%
Knightsbridge Tankers	NASDAQ: NVLCCF	9%
Nordic American Tankers	NYSE: NAT	9%

If you do decide to invest in the global oil-shipping business, I recommend digging deeper into a target company's operations. You can find most of the information you need in a company's annual report (Form 10K) or quarterly report (Form 10Q). You can obtain additional information through third parties, such as analyst reports.

One of the best-kept secrets in this industry is the high dividend payout these companies issue. I'm a huge fan of dividends because they provide you with certainty in an uncertain investment world. And oil tanker stocks offer some of the highest dividend payouts out there. Table 6-2 gives you a group of shipping company stocks that offer some remarkable dividend payouts.

Calculating dividend payouts can be tricky because a company isn't obligated to give back money to shareholders in the form of dividends. Some companies pay out high dividends one year but not the next; for others, paying dividends may be only a one-time event. One way to determine future dividend payouts is to examine the company's dividend payout history. Any good stock screener should have this information handy. I find that the Yahoo! Finance Web site does the job: www.finance.yahoo.com.

Swimming with sharks: Avoiding industry risk

As with most aspects of commodities, tanker spot rates and fixed rates, which provide the bulk of a shipping company's revenue stream, are highly cyclical. It's not extraordinary for shipping rates to fluctuate by 60 or 70 percent on a daily basis.

So how do you protect yourself from these extreme price volatilities? One way to hedge your position is to invest in one of the large oil tanker stocks I mention in the preceding section. These companies have been in the business a long time and have substantial experience managing these wild price swings.

Another factor to consider is global economic growth. The oil-shipping industry depends on a strong global economy with a healthy appetite for crude oil and crude oil products. If the global economy is thrown into a recession, you can expect the tanker stocks to take a hit. With everything else equal, if the world demand for oil products slows down, I recommend getting out of these tanker stocks.

If you're a more adventurous investor, you always have the option to short the stock of companies you know aren't going to do well. You can short a company's stock through various means, such as buying a put option or even selling a call option. I discuss short selling in Chapter 13.

Part III

Metals and Agricultural Products

Four Top Uses for Gold

- ✔ **Dentistry:** Gold is alloyed with other metals, such as silver, copper, and platinum, to create dental fixtures.

- ✔ **Electronics:** Because of its ability to efficiently conduct electricity, gold is used as a semiconductor in circuit boards and integrated boards in everything from cellphones and TVs to missiles.

- ✔ **Jewelry:** Used as an ornament and in jewelry since ancient times. Jewelry is the most important consumer use of gold in the world, accounting for more than 70 percent of total consumption.

- ✔ **Monetary:** Many central banks hold reserves of gold. Gold is one of the only commodities that's held in its physical form for investment purposes by the investing public. Also traditionally used in coinage, though not so much anymore.

Get some background on two major commodities exchanges, the Chicago Board of Trade and the Chicago Mercantile Exchange, at www.dummies.com/extras/investingincommodities.

In this part . . .

- ✓ Invest in gold, silver, and platinum
- ✓ Make money in steel, aluminum, copper, palladium, zinc, and nickel
- ✓ Check out mining companies and conglomerates and investigate their investment suitability
- ✓ Invest in coffee, cocoa, sugar, orange juice, corn, wheat, soybeans, cattle, hogs, and, last but not least, good old pork bellies

Chapter 7

Investing in the Precious: Gold, Silver, and Platinum

*M*etallurgy and civilization go hand in hand. Mankind's ability to control metals enabled us to develop modern society and civilization. As a matter of fact, human prehistory is classified by using a three-age system based on the ability to control metals: the Stone Age, the Bronze Age, and the Iron Age. Societies that have mastered the use of metals in weaponry and tool making have been able to thrive and survive. Societies without this ability have faced extinction.

Similarly, investors who have been able to master the fundamentals of the metals markets have been handsomely rewarded. In this chapter, I introduce you to the fascinating world of precious metals, which includes gold, silver, and platinum. These metals can play a role in your portfolio because of their precious metal status, their ability to act as a store of value, and their potential to provide a hedge against inflation. In this chapter, you discover all you need to know to incorporate precious metals into your portfolio.

As a general rule, metals are classified into two broad categories: *precious metals* and *base metals*. This classification is based on a metal's resistance to corrosion and oxidation: Precious metals have a high resistance to corrosion, whereas base metals (covered in Chapter 8) have a lower tolerance.

Investing in companies that mine precious metals — or any other commodity, for that matter — doesn't give you direct exposure to the price fluctuations of that commodity. You need to be familiar with the fluctuations and patterns of the equity markets to profit from this investment methodology. You also need to consider any external factors that impact the performance of the company, such as management effectiveness, total debt levels, areas of operation, and other metrics that are specific to companies. That said, investing in the equity markets still gives you access to the commodities markets.

Going for the Gold

Perhaps no other metal — or commodity — in the world has the cachet and prestige of gold. For centuries, gold has been coveted and valued for its unique metallurgical characteristics. It was such a desirable commodity that it developed monetary applications, and a number of currencies were based on the value of gold. In 1944, for example, 44 of the world's richest countries (including the United States) decided to peg their currencies to the yellow metal, in what is known as the Bretton Woods Agreement. Although President Nixon removed the dollar from the gold standard in 1971, many countries still use gold as a global currency benchmark.

In addition, gold has a number of applications in industry and jewelry that have resulted in increased demand for this precious metal.

When I wrote *Commodities For Dummies* (Wiley) in 2006, I strongly urged investors to invest in gold for the long term. Back when I first made this recommendation, gold was trading in the range of $500 per ounce; the current gold price as of this writing in 2015 is $1,350 per ounce. Investors who acted on my recommendation would now be up approximately 300 percent at a time of increased volatility and reduced returns in the global market indexes.

My outlook for gold during the next five years remains positive. Overall, I believe demand for gold will continue to increase, especially as a store of value, driven in part by the weakening paper currency environment that's a result of expansionary monetary policy in the Organization for Economic Cooperation and Development (OECD) countries. As paper currencies come under increased pressure, expect demand for gold to increase. Of course, no investment goes up in a straight line, so expect a bumpy ride and some periods of big pullbacks along the way. For more on my views on gold and the world economy, visit `www.commodities-investors.com`.

Getting to know the gold standard

The increased demand for gold is linked to a number of reasons. To profit from this increased demand, you need to be familiar with the fundamentals of the gold market. I go through these market fundamentals in this section.

First, you need to know what gold is used for. You may not be surprised to hear that jewelry accounts for a large portion of gold demand. However, did you know that dentistry also represents a significant portion of the gold market? Take a look at some of the uses of gold:

- ✔ **Dentistry:** Because gold resists corrosion, it has wide application in dentistry. It's alloyed with other metals, such as silver, copper, and platinum, to create dental fixtures.

- ✔ **Electronics:** Because of its ability to efficiently conduct electricity, gold is a popular metal in electronics. It's used as a semiconductor in circuit boards and integrated boards in everything from cellphones and TVs to missiles.

- ✔ **Jewelry:** Since man first discovered it thousands of years ago, gold has been used as an ornament and in jewelry. The ancient Egyptian King Tutankhamen was so enamored with gold that he was buried in a gold coffin. Today jewelry is the most important consumer use of gold in the world, accounting for more than 70 percent of total consumption.

- ✔ **Monetary:** Many central banks hold reserves of gold. In addition, gold is one of the only commodities that's held in its physical form for investment purposes by the investing public (see the "Let's get physical" section, later in this chapter). Another monetary use of gold, aside from central bank reserves and investor portfolios, is the use of gold in coinage. In countries such as Canada and South Africa, some gold coins are actually legal tender.

What makes gold valuable

Why is gold such an important metal? These traits can help you understand where gold derives its value:

- ✔ **Ductility:** Gold is a very ductile metal. In metallurgy, *ductility* measures how much a metal can be drawn out into a wire. For example, 1 ounce of gold can be converted into more than 50 miles of gold wire! This gold wire can then be applied in electronics and used as an electric conductor.

- ✔ **Malleability:** Pure gold (24 karat) is a very malleable metal and is prized by craftsmen around the world who shape it into jewelry and other objects of beauty. One ounce of gold can be transformed into more than 96 square feet of gold sheet!

- ✔ **Quasi-indestructibility:** Gold has high resistance levels and doesn't easily corrode. Corrosive agents such as oxygen and heat have almost no effect on gold, which can retain its luster over long periods of time (think thousands of years). The only chemical that can affect gold is cyanide, which dissolves gold.

- ✔ **Rarity:** Gold is one of the rarest natural resources on earth. Most people don't realize this, but only about 150,000 tons of gold have ever been produced since humans first began mining gold more than 6,000 years ago. To give you an idea of how little that is, all the gold in the world wouldn't even fill up four Olympic-size swimming pools! And because most gold is recycled and never destroyed, a majority of gold is still in use today. About 15 percent of gold is recycled every year.

How to measure gold

Gold, like most metals, is measured and weighed in *troy ounces.* One troy ounce is the equivalent of 31.10 grams. (Despite the common misperception, the troy ounce does not take its name from the mythic ancient Greek city of Troy. It's named after the French town of Troyes, which was an important center of trade and commerce with a thriving precious metals market during the Middle Ages.) When you buy gold for investment purposes, such as through an exchange-traded fund (ETF) or gold certificates, troy ounces is the measurement of choice.

When you want to refer to large quantities of gold, such as the amount of gold a bank holds in reserves or the amount of gold produced in a mine, the unit of measurement you use is *metric tons.* One metric ton is equal to 32,150 troy ounces.

If you've bought gold jewelry, you may have come across the following measurement: karats. *Karats* (sometimes spelled *carats*) measure the purity of gold. The purest form of gold is 24-karat gold (24K). Everything below that number denotes that the gold is alloyed, or mixed, with another metal.

Table 7-1 shows what the different numbers of karats translate to in terms of gold's purity.

Table 7-1	Purity of Gold, Measured in Karats
Karats	*Purity (%)*
24K	100
22K	91.67
18K	75
14K	58.3
10K	41.67
9K	37.5

If you buy physical gold for either adornment (jewelry) or investment (gold coins/bars), you want to get the purest form of gold, 24K. If you can't get 24K gold, aim to get the purest form of gold you can get your hands on. Remember that the purer the gold, the higher its value. Pure gold (24K) is always a yellow color. However, you've probably encountered white gold or even red gold — these other colors are created by alloying gold with metals such as nickel or palladium for a white color or with copper to create *red gold.* By definition, white and red gold aren't pure gold.

Whereas purity measures how precious gold is in a percentage basis, *fineness* measures gold's purity expressed as a whole number. Fortunately, fineness and purity are so similar that gold with 91.67 percent purity has a fineness of 0.9167.

Good as gold: Finding ways to invest in gold

In this section, I introduce you to the different ways you can invest in gold: physical gold, gold ETFs, gold-mining companies, and gold futures contracts.

Let's get physical

Gold is unlike any other commodity because it's one of the few commodities that can be physically stored to have its value preserved or increased over periods of time. One investment method unique to gold is to actually buy it — hard, physical gold. You can purchase gold bars, bullion, and coins and store them in a safe location as an investment. Perhaps no other commodity offers you this unique opportunity. (Storing physical coal or uranium for investment purposes just doesn't work, believe me!) In some countries, folks actually buy gold jewelry for the dual purpose of adornment and investment. You can get your hands on these different forms of gold:

✔ **Gold bars:** Gold bars have an undeniable allure. In pop culture, for example, gold is usually depicted as large gold bars. Think of the movies *Goldfinger* and *Die Hard 3,* for instance. Much more than great movie props, gold bars are a great investment. Whereas gold coins are more suited for smaller purchases, gold bars are ideal if you're interested in purchasing larger quantities of gold. Despite popular depictions, gold bars come in all shapes and sizes. They can be as small as 1 gram or as large as 400 troy ounces. Despite the size, most gold bars are high quality, with a fineness of 0.999 and above (24 karats). For a comprehensive listing of gold bars, I recommend *The Industry Catalogue of Gold Bars Worldwide,* which you can find at www.grendon.com.au/goldbarscat. htm. Perhaps the only drawback of gold bars is their size, which makes them harder (and more expensive) to store.

Gold *bullion* is nothing more than large gold bars.

✔ **Gold certificates:** Gold certificates are a hybrid instrument that allows you to own physical gold without actually taking possession of it. As the name implies, gold certificates certify that you own a certain amount of gold, which is usually stored in a safe location by the authority that issues the gold certificates. Owning gold certificates is my favorite way of owning physical gold because they're safe and easy to store. When you own gold bars or coins, safety is always a concern — someone could literally steal your gold. Storage is another concern, particularly if you have large quantities of the stuff, because it can end up costing you a lot to store your gold (such as in a bank vault or personal safe). The gold standard of gold certificates is the Perth Mint Certificate Program (PMCP).

The Perth Mint, Australia's oldest and most important mint, administers the PMCP. At one point, the Perth Mint had as much gold as Fort Knox. The PMCP is the only certificate program guaranteed by a government — in this case, the government of Western Australia. The PMCP issues you a certificate and stores your gold in a secure government vault. You may retrieve or sell your gold at any point. For more on this program, check out the Perth Mint's Web site, at www.perthmint.com.au.

✔ **Gold coins:** One of the easiest ways to invest in physical gold is to buy gold coins. I like gold coins because they give you a lot of bang for your buck. Unlike large gold bars, gold coins allow you to purchase the yellow metal in smaller quantities and units. This flexibility offers two advantages: First, you don't have to put up as much money to buy a gold coin, compared to buying a gold bar. Second, if you want to sell part of your gold holdings, you can easily sell five gold coins and keep five — that's not possible when you have only one gold bar. Another reason I like gold coins is that you can easily and safely store them; they're more discreet than having large gold bullion. The third reason I like gold coins is that they're issued by a federal government and instantly recognized as such; in some countries (Canada and South Africa), they're even considered legal tender. I list the most popular types of gold coins, by country of issuance, here:

- **Gold eagle:** The U.S. government issues the gold eagle coin; it has the full backing of Congress and the U.S. Mint. It comes in various sizes, including 1 ounce, 1/2 ounce, 1/4 ounce, and 1/10 ounce. At 22K, the gold eagle coin is a high-quality coin that you can actually use to fund an IRA account.

- **Gold Krugerrand:** The gold Krugerrand is issued by the South African government and is one of the oldest gold coins issued in the world. It has a fineness of 0.916.

- **Gold maple leaf:** You guessed it — the Canadian government backs the gold maple leaf. It's issued by the Royal Canadian Mint and, at 24K, is the purest gold coin on the market.

If you want to purchase gold coins, bars, or even certificates, you need to go through a gold dealer. One gold dealer I recommend is Kitco (www.kitco.com). Before you do business with any gold dealer, though, find out as much information about the business (and business history) as possible. You can check out different gold dealers by going through the Better Business Bureau, at www.bbb.org.

Gold ETFs

Exchange-traded funds that offer exposure to commodities are a popular investment gateway for folks who don't want to mess around with futures contracts, as I explain in Chapter 12. Signaling gold's importance, one of the first commodity ETFs to hit the market is, you guessed it, a gold ETF. Currently, you can choose from two gold ETFs:

- ✔ **iShares COMEX Gold Trust (AMEX: IAU):** The iShares gold ETF holds a little more than 1.3 million ounces of gold in its vaults. The per-unit price of the ETF seeks to reflect the current market price in the spot market of the ETF gold.

- ✔ **StreetTracks Gold Shares (NYSE: GLD):** The StreetTracks gold ETF is the largest gold ETF on the market today. Launched in late 2004, it holds about 12 million ounces of physical gold in secured locations. The price per ETF unit is calculated based on the average of the bid/ask spread in the gold spot market. This fund is a good way to get exposure to physical gold without actually owning it.

Find out about the fees and expenses associated with each of the ETFs mentioned. These ETFs have to pay a number of entities to actually hold physical gold, so inquire about any storage fees. These fees are in addition to the general fund expenses, such as registration and administration fees. Carefully consider all expenses and fees, because they have a direct impact on your bottom line. (For more on ETFs, turn to Chapter 12.)

Because both the StreetTracks and iShares ETFs track the price of gold on the spot market, their performance is remarkably similar — at times, it's actually identical. Therefore, if you can't decide between the two, I recommend StreetTracks because it holds more physical gold and, more important, offers you more liquidity than the iShares ETF.

Stocks in gold companies

Another way to get exposure to gold is to invest in gold-mining companies. A number of companies specialize in mining, processing, and distributing this precious metal. I recommend these companies:

- ✔ **AngloGold Ashanti Ltd. (NYSE: AU):** AngloGold, which is listed in five different stock exchanges around the world, is a truly global gold company. Based in South Africa, it operates more than 20 mines and has significant operations in Africa and South America, particularly in South Africa, Namibia, Tanzania, Ghana, Mali, Brazil, Argentina, and Peru, which all have major gold deposits. It has additional operations in Australia and North America. AngloGold is a wholly owned subsidiary of Anglo-American, the global mining giant (which I cover in Chapter 9).

- ✔ **Barrick Gold Corporation (NYSE: ABX):** Barrick is a Canadian company with headquarters in Toronto. It's a premier player in the gold-mining industry and has operations in Argentina, Australia, Canada, Chile, Papua New Guinea, Peru, South Africa, Tanzania, and the United States. It also has a foothold in the potentially lucrative Central Asian market, where it has joint operations in Mongolia, Russia, and Turkey. Another reason I like Barrick is that it has one of the lowest production costs per ounce of gold in the industry.

- ✔ **New Gold, Inc. (AMEX: NGD):** New Gold is a junior gold-mining company headquartered in Vancouver, British Columbia. It was founded in 2005 and currently operates three highly profitable mines in California, Mexico, and Australia; the cash costs per ounce for each of these mines are in the industry lows, translating into high margins. In addition, NGD is in the process of exploiting two additional mines, one in Canada and the other in Chile, two mining-friendly jurisdictions. The management team's successful track record in making acquisitions

and operating mines makes this an indispensable investment for anyone looking for exposure to gold markets.

✔ **Newmont Mining Corporation (NYSE: NEM):** Newmont,
headquartered in Colorado, is one of the largest gold-
mining companies in the world. It has operations in
Australia, Bolivia, Canada, Indonesia, Peru, the United
States (Nevada and California), and Uzbekistan. It's
actually the largest gold producer in South America.
Additionally, it has exploration programs in Ghana that
may be very promising for the company. If you're looking
for a truly global and diversified gold producer with real
growth potential, you can't go wrong with Newmont.

A number of other mining companies have gold-mining operations that are part of a general mining program that includes
other metals, such as silver and copper. I selected these companies because their sphere of operations revolves almost
exclusively around gold mining.

The performance of these companies isn't directly proportional to the spot or future price of gold. These companies
don't give you the direct exposure to gold that gold certificates or bars do, for example. Also, by investing in these
stocks, you're exposing yourself to regulatory, managerial,
and operational factors.

Gold contracts

Gold futures contracts give you a direct way to invest in gold
through the futures markets. You can choose from two gold
futures contracts that are widely traded in the United States
(see Chapter 13 for the goods on futures contracts):

✔ **CME/CBOT Mini-Gold (CBOT: YG):** Launched in 2004,
this gold contract, trading in the CBOT section of the
Chicago Mercantile Exchange (CME), is a relative new-
comer to the North American gold futures market.
However, it's a popular contract because you can trade
it online through the CME's electronic trading platform.
In addition, at a contract size of 33.2 troy ounces, the
mini is popular with investors and traders who prefer to
trade this smaller-size contract than the larger 100-ounce
contract.

↙ **CME/CBOT E-Micro Gold (CBOT: MGC):** Launched in 2010, this gold contract trades on the COMEX section of the Chicago Mercantile Exchange (CME). The contract is relatively new, and popularity has been growing each month with its electronic execution traded on the CME Globex platform. At a contract size of 10 troy ounces, the E-Micro is popular with investors and traders who prefer to trade a smaller size contract than the Mini-Gold 33.2 troy ounce.

↙ **CME/COMEX Gold (COMEX: GC):** The COMEX gold futures contract was the first such contract to hit the market in the United States (back in the 1970s). It's traded on the COMEX division of the CME, and it's the most liquid gold contract in the world. It's used primarily by large commercial consumers and producers, such as jewelry manufacturers and mining companies, for price-hedging purposes. However, you can also purchase the contract for investment purposes. Each contract represents 100 troy ounces of gold.

When investing in the futures markets, always trade in the most liquid markets. *Liquidity* is an indication of the number of contracts traded on a regular basis. The higher the liquidity, the more likely you are to find a buyer or seller to close out or open a position. You can get information on the volume and open interest of contracts traded in the futures markets through the Commodity Futures Trading Commission (CFTC) Web site, at www.cftc.gov.

Investing in Silver

Silverware and jewelry aren't the only uses for silver. As a matter of fact, silverware is only a small portion of the silver market. A large portion of this precious metal goes toward industrial uses, such as conducting electricity; creating bearings; and welding, soldering, and brazing (the process by which metals are permanently joined together). Because of its numerous practical applications and its status as a precious metal, investing in silver can bolster your portfolio. In this section, I introduce you to the ins and outs of the silver market and then show you how to actually include silver in your portfolio.

Checking out the big picture on the silver screen

Silver has a number of uses that make it an attractive investment. This list details the most important ones, which account for more than 95 percent of total demand for silver:

- ✔ **Industrial:** The industrial sector is the single largest consumer of silver products, accounting for almost 50 percent of total silver consumption in 2015. Silver has a number of applications in the industrial sector, including creating control switches for electrical appliances and connecting electronic circuit boards. Because it's a good electrical conductor, silver will keep playing an important role in the industrial sector.

- ✔ **Jewelry and silverware:** Many people believe (incorrectly) that the largest consumer of silver is the jewelry industry. Although silver does play a large role in creating jewelry and silverware, demand from this sector accounted for 25 percent of total silver consumption in 2015.

- ✔ **Photography:** The photographic industry used to be a major consumer of silver, accounting for about 20 percent of total consumption as late as 2006. In photography, silver is compounded with halogens to form *silver halide,* which is used in photographic film. With the rise of digital cameras, which don't use silver halide, becoming more popular than traditional cameras, photography demand for silver went from 20 percent in 2006 to less than 7 percent in 2015.

Monitor the commercial activity in each of these market segments and look for signs of strength or weakness, because a demand increase or decrease in one of these markets, such as photography, will have a direct impact on the price of silver.

Knowing where the silver comes from is always important to an investor, so I list the top producers of silver in the world in Table 7-2.

Table 7-2	Top Silver Producers, 2015
Country	*Production (Millions of Ounces)*
Peru	124
Mexico	105
China	89
Australia	52
Bolivia	42
Russia	42
Chile	41
Poland	40
United States	39
Kazakhstan	20

If you're interested in finding out more about silver and its investment possibilities, the Silver Institute, a trade association for silver producers and consumers, maintains a comprehensive database on the silver market. Its Web site is www. silverinstitute.org.

Getting a sliver of silver in your portfolio

Silver can play an important role in your portfolio. Because of its precious metal status, you can use it as a hedge against inflation and to preserve part of your portfolio's value. In addition, because it has important industrial applications, you can use it for capital appreciation opportunities. Whether for capital preservation or appreciation, I believe any portfolio has room for some exposure to silver. In this section, I introduce you to the different ways you can invest in silver.

Buying physical silver

One of the unique characteristics of silver is that you can invest in it by actually buying the stuff, as you can buy gold coins and bars for investment purposes. Most dealers that sell gold generally offer silver coins and bars as well.

✔ **100-ounce silver bar:** If you're interested in something substantial, you can buy a 100-ounce silver bar. Before buying it, check the bar to make sure that it's pure silver (you want 99 percent purity or above).

✔ **Silver maple coins:** These coins, products of the Royal Canadian Mint, are the standard for silver coins around the world. Each coin represents 1 ounce of silver and has a purity of 99.99 percent, making it the most pure silver coin on the market.

The term *sterling silver* refers to a specific silver alloy that contains 92.5 percent silver and 7.5 percent copper (other base metals are occasionally used as well). Pure silver is sometimes alloyed with another metal, such as copper, to make it stronger and more durable. Just remember that if you're considering silver jewelry as an investment, sterling silver won't give you as much value in the long term as pure silver.

Buying the silver ETF

One of the most convenient ways of investing in silver is to go through an exchange-traded fund (ETF). Until recently, no ETFs tracked silver. However, Barclays Global Investors (a subsidiary of the investment bank) launched an ETF through its iShares program in April 2006 to track the price of silver. The iShares Silver Trust (AMEX: SLV) holds silver bullion in a vault and seeks to mirror the spot price of that silver based on current market prices. This new silver ETF is a testament to the increased demand by investors to include silver in their portfolios.

Looking at silver-mining companies

Another alternative investment route is to go through companies that mine silver. Although some of the larger mining companies (covered in Chapter 9) have silver-mining operations, you can get more direct exposure to the silver markets by investing in companies that specialize in mining this precious metal. These companies may not be household names, but they're a potentially good investment nevertheless. This list details a couple companies that focus exclusively on mining silver:

✔ **Pan American Silver Corporation (NASDAQ: PAAS):** Pan American Silver, based in Vancouver, has extensive operations in the Americas. It operates six mines in some of the most prominent locations in the world, including

Bolivia, Mexico, and Peru. If you're interested in a well-managed company to get exposure to Latin American silver mines, you won't go wrong with Pan American Silver.

✔ **Silver Wheaton Corp. (NYSE: SLW):** Silver Wheaton is one of the only mining companies that generates all its revenues from silver-mining activity. Whereas other mining companies may have smaller interests in other metals, Silver Wheaton focuses exclusively on developing and mining silver. It has operations in geographically diverse areas that stretch from Mexico to Sweden. If you're looking for a geographically diverse company to give you direct access to silver-mining activities, Silver Wheaton is your best bet.

Checking out silver futures contracts

Similar to gold futures, silver futures contracts give you the most direct access to the silver market. Following are the most liquid silver futures contracts:

✔ **CBOT Mini-Silver (CBOT: YI):** The Mini-Silver contract that trades on the CBOT division of the CME represents a stake in 1,000 troy ounces of silver with a purity of 99.9 percent. This contract is available for electronic trading.

✔ **COMEX Silver (COMEX: SI):** The COMEX silver contract is the standard futures contract for silver. It's traded on the COMEX division of the CME and represents 5,000 troy ounces of silver per contract.

Bling Bling: Investing in Platinum

Platinum, sometimes referred to as "the rich man's gold," is one of the rarest and most precious metals in the world. Perhaps no other metal or commodity carries the same cachet as platinum, and for good reason: It's by far the rarest metal in the world. If you put all the platinum that has ever been mined into an Olympic-size swimming pool, that platinum wouldn't even cover your ankles! Whereas precious and base metals such as gold and copper have been exploited for thousands of years, man's interest in platinum developed only in the 17th century, when the Conquistadors discovered relatively large amounts of the metal in South America. Platinum was soon discovered to have superior characteristics to most metals: It's more resistant to corrosion, doesn't oxidize in the air, and has stable chemical properties. Because of these characteristics, platinum is a highly desirable metal and can play an important role in your portfolio.

Platinum is also the name of the group of metals that includes platinum, palladium, osmium, ruthenium, rhodium, and iridium. In this section, I talk about the metal, not the group of metals, although I cover palladium in Chapter 8.

Gathering platinum facts and figures

Deposits of platinum ore are extremely scarce and, more important, are geographically concentrated in a few regions around the globe, primarily in South Africa, Russia, and North America. South Africa has the largest deposits of platinum in the world and, by some accounts, may contain up to 90 percent of the world's total reserve estimates. Russia is also a large player in the production of platinum, currently accounting for 20 percent of total global production (2010 figures). North America also contains some commercially viable platinum mines, located mostly in Montana.

So who uses platinum? Platinum has several uses, but these are the most important:

- ✔ **Catalytic converters:** You may be surprised to find out not only that platinum is used in catalytic converters in transportation vehicles, but also that this accounts for more than 45 percent of total platinum demand. Platinum's unique characteristics make it a suitable metal in the production of these pollution-reducing devices. As environmental fuel standards become more stringent, expect the demand from this sector to increase.

- ✔ **Industrial:** Because it's a great conductor of heat and electricity, platinum has wide applications in industry. It's used in creating everything from personal computer hard drives to fiber-optic cables. Despite its relative value, platinum will continue to be used for industrial purposes.

> ✓ **Jewelry:** At one point, jewelry accounted for more than
> 50 percent of total demand for platinum. Although that
> number has decreased, the jewelry industry is still a
> major purchaser of platinum metals for use in highly
> prized jewelry.

A change in demand from one of these industries will affect
the price of platinum. The International Platinum Association
maintains an updated database of the uses of platinum. Check
out its Web site for more information on platinum supply and
demand, at `www.platinuminfo.net`.

Going platinum

Platinum's unique characteristics as a highly sought-after
precious metal with industrial applications make it an ideal
investment. Fortunately, you can invest in platinum in a
number of ways. I list a couple of these methods in the following sections.

Platinum futures contract

The most direct way of investing in platinum is to go through
the futures markets. The Chicago Mercantile Exchange (CME)
offers a platinum futures contract. Due to platinum's uses in
industry and a store of value, it has experienced increased
demand from investors; however, platinum is also a highly
sensitive trading instrument and tends to react drastically to
any price shocks, as was the case during the Global Financial
Crisis of 2008. Platinum can be subject to wide price swings,
so it's not for the buy-and-hold investor; taking advantage of
this opportunity requires quick and tactical trading strategies.

The CME platinum futures contract represents 50 troy ounces
of platinum and is available for trading electronically. It trades
under the ticker symbol PL.

Platinum-mining companies

Check out a couple companies that give you direct exposure
to platinum-mining activities:

> ✓ **Anglo-American PLC (NASDAQ: AAUK):** Anglo-American
> is a diversified mining company that has activities in
> gold, silver, platinum, and other precious metals. I recom-
> mend Anglo-American because it has significant interests

in South African platinum mines, the largest mines in the world. If you're looking for an indirect exposure to South Africa's platinum mining industry, Anglo-American does the trick.

✔ **Stillwater Mining Company (NYSE: SWC):** Stillwater Mining is headquartered in Billings, Montana, and owns the rights to the Stillwater mining complex in Montana, which contains one of the largest commercially viable platinum mines in North America. This option is a good play on North American platinum-mining activities.

Chapter 8

All About that Base: Investing in Steel, Aluminum, Copper, and Other Metals

Steel, aluminum, and copper may not be as glamorous as their precious counterparts — gold, silver, and platinum, covered in Chapter 7 — but they're perhaps even more precious to the global economy. Without these metals, which are literally the building blocks of modern societies, life as you and I know it wouldn't exist. Buildings couldn't be built without steel, cars wouldn't be as lightweight and efficient without aluminum, and you probably wouldn't be able to get any electricity in your home without copper, which is the electrical conductor of choice. Due in part to rapid industrialization in China (which happens to be the largest steel producer), India, and other leading developing countries, demand for these three building block metals is strong and will remain robust for the medium to long term. The future looks bright for these metals.

Other metals — the precious metal palladium and the industrial metals zinc and nickel — are important components of the metals complex in their own right: palladium because of its precious metal status and as a part of the *platinum group of metals* (PGM), and nickel and zinc for their wide use in industry. These metals may not get much attention from the financial press, but you still need to consider including them in your portfolio: They're essential building blocks of the global economy.

I outline the market characteristics of each of these metals so that you can determine whether they're right for you.

Building a Portfolio as Strong As Steel

The development of steel, alongside iron, changed the course of human history. In fact, the last stage of prehistoric times, the Iron Age, is so named because humans mastered the iron- and steel-making processes. This development allowed societies to build tools and weapons, which speeded advancements in construction and technology. Steel was responsible for another revolution in the 19th century: the Industrial Revolution. Today, in a high-tech world dominated by software and technological gadgets, this age-old metal is still as reliable as ever. In fact, steel is making a resurgence as advanced developing countries — China, India, and Brazil — barrel down a path toward rapid industrialization not unlike the one the West experienced in the 19th century. *Steel,* which is iron alloyed with other compounds (usually carbon), is still the most widely produced metal in the world.

Steel is measured in *metric tons,* sometimes abbreviated as MT. For *global* production and consumption figures, *million metric tons* (MMT) is used.

Steely facts

Before I introduce the best ways to invest in steel, take a look at the dynamics of the broader steel industry. China dominates steel production, with generous subsidies in place for its steel manufacturers. China now produces three times more steel than Japan, the second-largest producer. For a long time, the United States was the number one producer of steel, but its dominance eroded largely because of competition from Asia (especially China and Japan) and partly for internal reasons (such as the high costs of running a steel mill in the United States). The United States is still an important player in the steel industry; other countries worth mentioning include Russia, Germany, and South Korea. In Table 8-1, I list the top steel producers in the world in 2015. To put things in perspective, total global steel production in 2015 stood at 1,220 MMT.

Table 8-1 Top Steel-Producing Countries, 2015

Country	Production (Million Metric Tons)
China	620
Japan	90
United States	75
Russia	60
India	55
South Korea	45
Germany	30
Ukraine	25
Brazil	25

Source: International Iron and Steel Institute

If you're interested in exploring additional statistical information relating to steel production and manufacturing, I recommend checking out the following resources:

- **Association for Iron and Steel Technology:** www.aist.org
- **International Iron and Steel Institute:** www.worldsteel.org
- **Iron and Steel Statistics Bureau:** www.issb.co.uk

Investing in steel companies

Although futures contracts are available for everything from crude oil to coffee, there's no underlying futures contract for steel. However, a number of exchanges have expressed interest in developing a steel futures contract, so keep an eye out for such a development.

For now, the best way to get exposure to steel is to invest in companies that produce steel, specifically globally integrated steel companies. The companies listed in Table 8-2 are global leaders in the steel industry.

Table 8-2   Top Steel-Producing Companies, 2015

Company	Production (Million Metric Tons)
ArcelorMittal (worldwide)	78
Baosteel (China)	31
POSCO (South Korea)	30
Nippon Steel (Japan)	27
JFE Group (Japan)	27
Jiangsu Shagang (China)	21
Tata Steel (India)	20
Ansteel (China)	20
Severstal (Russia)	17
Evraz (Russia)	15

Source: International Iron and Steel Institute

The companies in Table 8-2 are the leaders, but not all are available for investment. Some of them are private, and others trade on foreign exchanges that don't issue *American Depository Receipts* (ADRs). (Turn to Chapter 9 for more on ADRs, which essentially allow you to invest in foreign companies through U.S. stock exchanges.) The following list represents good investments that not only are the best-run companies, but also display the greatest potential for future market dominance:

> ✔ **Arcelor-Mittal (NYSE: MT):** Arcelor-Mittal resulted when the Indian company Mittal acquired the European Arcelor in 2006, in one of the biggest consolidation plays the industry has ever seen. Combining the number one and number two steel producers has created a dominant leader with output, almost double that of its nearest competitor. If you're looking for broad exposure to the steel industry, you can't go wrong with Arcelor-Mittal.

✔ **Gerdau (NYSE: GGB):** Gerdau is a Brazilian vertically integrated steel producer with operations across several countries. Gerdau is a dominant player in the long steel category, with mills in Brazil, Argentina, Mexico, Colombia, and the United States. It brought in a net income of more than $800 million in 2009, so you can remain confident that this company will generate long-term value for its shareholders.

✔ **Nucor Corp. (NYSE: NUE):** The American steel industry remains a robust competitor on the global stage, despite the dominance of Asian (particularly Chinese) companies. Nucor operates almost exclusively in the United States; if you're interested in getting exposure to the American steel market, consider investing in it. Nucor is also one of the only companies to operate *minimills* domestically, which many argue are more cost efficient than the traditional blast furnaces.

✔ **U.S. Steel (NYSE: X):** U.S. Steel, which was formed as a result of the consolidation of Andrew Carnegie's steel holdings in the early 20th century, is one of the oldest and largest steel companies in the world. By itself, U.S. Steel represents the whole history of the modern steel industry. At one point, it was the largest producer of steel in the world. Although it has scaled down its operations, it's still a significant player in the industry today. U.S. Steel is involved in all aspects of the steel-making process, from iron ore mining and processing to the marketing of finished products.

Aluminum: Illuminating the Details

Aluminum is one of the most ubiquitous metals of modern society. Not just aluminum soda cans account for its widespread use — aluminum is also used in transportation (cars, trucks, trains, and airplanes), construction, and electrical power lines, to name just a few end uses. As a matter of fact, aluminum is the second most widely used metal in the world, right after steel. Because of its indispensability, you need to make room to include this metal in your portfolio. In this section, I show you how to do just that.

Aluminum is generally measured in *metric tons* (MT).

Just the aluminum facts

Aluminum is a lightweight metal that's resistant to corrosion. Because of these characteristics, it's widely used to create a number of products, from cars to jets. Consider a few items made out of aluminum:

- ✔ **Construction:** Aluminum has industrial uses as well, including a role in the construction of buildings, oil pipelines, and even bridges. Building constructors are attracted to it because it's lightweight, durable, and sturdy.

- ✔ **Packaging:** Almost a quarter of aluminum is used to create aluminum wrap and foil, along with beverage cans and rivets.

- ✔ **Transportation:** Aluminum is used to create the body, axles, and, in some cases, engines of cars. In addition, large commercial aircrafts are built using aluminum because of its light weight and sturdiness.

Table 8-3 breaks down total aluminum consumption by sector.

Table 8-3   Aluminum Consumption by Sector, 2015

Industry	Aluminum Consumption (% of Total)
Transportation	26
Packaging	22
Construction	22
Electrical	8
Machinery	8
Consumer goods	7
Miscellaneous uses	7

Source: London Metal Exchange (LME)

If you're interested in finding out more about the aluminum industry, I recommend checking out the following organizations:

- ✔ **The Aluminum Association:** www.aluminum.org
- ✔ **aluNET International:** www.alunet.net

> ✔ **International Aluminium Institute:** www.world-
> aluminium.org

Aluminum futures

You can invest in aluminum through the futures markets. Previously, two major contracts for aluminum were available. The first one is through the London Metal Exchange (LME); the second one used to trade in the COMEX division of the New York Mercantile Exchange (NYMEX). However, the COMEX contract was delisted in 2009, after the Chicago Mercantile Exchange (CME) acquired the exchange. As a result, the go-to contract is now the LME.

The London Metal Exchange (LME) aluminum contract is the most liquid in the world. It represents a size of 25,000 tons, and its price is quoted in U.S. dollars.

Aluminum companies

Another way I recommend investing in aluminum is to invest in companies that produce and manufacture aluminum products. A few companies make the cut:

> ✔ **Alcoa (NYSE: AA):** Alcoa is the world leader in aluminum production. It's involved in all aspects of the aluminum industry and produces primary aluminum, fabricated aluminum, and alumina. The company has operations in more than 40 countries and services a large number of industries, from aerospace to construction. If you're looking to get the broadest exposure to the aluminum market, you can't go wrong with Alcoa.

> ✔ **Aluminum Corporation of China (NYSE: ACH):** As its name implies, ACH is primarily engaged in producing aluminum in the Chinese market. I recommend this company, which trades on the New York Stock Exchange (NYSE), because it gives you a foothold in the aluminum Chinese market, which may potentially be the biggest such market in the future. Besides this competitive advantage, ACH is a well-run company with profit margins that, during the writing of this book, were larger than 20 percent.

Bringing Copper into Your Metals Mix

Copper, the third most widely used metal in the world, has applications in many sectors, including construction, electricity conduction, and large-scale industrial projects. Copper is sought after because of its high electrical conductivity, resistance to corrosion, and malleability. Copper played a huge role during the Industrial Revolution and in connecting and wiring the modern world. Because of the current trends of industrialization and urbanization across the globe, demand for copper has been — and will remain — very strong, making it a good investment.

Quick copper facts

Copper is used for a variety of purposes, from building and construction to electrical wiring and engineering. To get a better idea of its wide usage, check out the breakdown of copper use by sector in Table 8-4.

Table 8-4   Copper Consumption by Sector, 2015

Sector	Copper Consumption (% of Total)
Building/construction	50
Engineering	24
Electrical	17
Transportation	7
Miscellaneous Uses	2

Source: Copper Development Association (CDA)

You probably come across items made from copper on a daily basis but may have never thought much about its ubiquity. These everyday items, among others, are made from copper:

- ✔ Artistic items (bronze statues such as the Statue of Liberty)
- ✔ Coinage (U.S. coins such as the quarter and the dime, which are more than 90 percent copper)
- ✔ Construction tubes, pipes, and fittings

- ✓ Doorknobs
- ✓ Electrical wiring
- ✓ High-speed Internet cables
- ✓ Industrial sleeve bearings
- ✓ Musical instruments (brass instruments such as the trumpet and the tuba)
- ✓ Plumbing tubes

Copper is often alloyed with other metals, usually with nickel and zinc. When copper and nickel are alloyed, the resulting metal is *bronze;* when copper is alloyed with zinc, it results in *brass.* Ironically, the U.S. penny, the only U.S. coin that's a reddish/brown color (the color of copper), is the only coin that uses only 2.5 percent copper — 97.5 percent of the penny is made from zinc. The other coins in U.S. currency, which are all silvery/white, contain more than 90 percent copper.

If you're interested in finding out more about copper usage, I recommend that you consult the Copper Development Association, at www.copper.org.

Copper futures contracts

Like most of the other important industrial metals, there's a futures market available for copper trading. Large industrial producers and consumers of the metal account for most of this market, although you also can use it for investment purposes. You have two copper contracts to choose from:

- ✓ **CME/COMEX Copper (COMEX: HG):** This copper contract trades in the COMEX division of the Chicago Mercantile Exchange (CME). COMEX copper, which trades during the current month and subsequent 23 calendar months, is traded both electronically and through the open outcry system. It represents 25,000 pounds of copper and trades under the symbol HG.

- ✓ **LME Copper (LME: CAD):** The copper contract on the London Metal Exchange (LME) accounts for more than 90 percent of total copper futures activity. It represents a lot size of 25 tons. *Note:* Because the LME is located in the United Kingdom, the British Financial Services Authority (FSA) regulates it.

Demand for copper from China, India, and other advanced developing countries is increasing, and that has put upward pressure on the price of copper.

Copper companies

Another investment vehicle I recommend is companies that specialize in mining and processing copper ore. The companies I list here are leaders in their industry and are involved in all aspects of the copper supply chain. The only drawback of investing in companies is that you don't get direct exposure to the price fluctuations of the metals. Still, these companies are a good option if you don't want to venture into the futures markets.

- ✔ **Freeport-McMoRan, Inc. (NYSE: FCX):** One of the reasons I like Freeport-McMoRan is that it's one of the lowest-cost producers of copper in the world. It has copper-mining and -smelting operations across the globe and has a significant presence in Indonesia and Papua New Guinea. The company specializes in producing highly concentrated copper ore, which it then sells on the open market. FCX also has some operations in gold and silver.

- ✔ **Phelps Dodge Corporation (NYSE: PD):** Founded in 1834, Phelps Dodge is one of the oldest mining companies in the United States. It's also one of the largest manufacturers and producers of copper and copper products in the world. The company has a global presence in copper mining, with operations in the United States, South Africa, the Philippines, and Peru, among others. Because of its size and experience in the industry, Phelps Dodge is in a good position to capitalize on increased demand for copper.

I cover copper companies in depth in Chapter 9. I also examine integrated and diversified mining companies, to help you design an investment strategy that effectively allows you to "buy the market."

Palladium: Metal for the New Millennium

Palladium, which belongs to the platinum group of metals (PGM), is a popular alternative to platinum in the automotive industry and the jewelry industry. Its largest use comes into play in the creation of pollution-reducing catalytic converters. Palladium's malleability and resistance to corrosion make it the perfect metal for such use. In addition, because palladium is less expensive per troy ounce than platinum ($624 per ounce versus $1,750 per ounce at the time of this writing in 2015), it's increasingly becoming the metal of choice in manufacturing these devices.

Aside from its usage in catalytic converters and jewelry, palladium is used in dentistry and electronics. Table 8-5 lists the main consumers of palladium.

Table 8-5   Palladium Consumption by Industry, 2015

Sector	% of Total
Auto industry (catalytic converters)	58
Jewelry	26
Electronics	17
Dentistry	15
Other	4

Source: U.S. Geological Survey

Palladium has benefited from more stringent fuel emission standards established by the _Environmental Protection Agency_ (EPA) and other international environmental organizations. When pollution-reducing regulation was established in the 1970s, demand for palladium skyrocketed as a direct result. All things equal, if emissions standards are further improved and require a new generation of catalytic converters, demand for palladium will increase. Another reason to be bullish on palladium is that the number of automobiles, trucks, and other vehicles equipped with platinum- and palladium-made catalytic converters is increasing, particularly in China. If you invest in palladium, keep an eye on automobile-manufacturing patterns.

Two countries essentially dominate the palladium market: Russia and South Africa. These two countries account for more than 85 percent of total palladium production, as you can see in Table 8-6.

Table 8-6   Top Palladium-Producing Countries, 2015

Country	Production (Million Ounces)
Russia	3.7
South Africa	2.4
North America	0.8
Zimbabwe	0.2
Other	0.25

Source: U.S. Geological Survey

Because these two countries dominate palladium production, any supply disruption from either country has a significant impact on palladium prices. Such was the case in early 2000, when the Russian government announced it would halt shipments of palladium and other platinum group metals for the year.

The Russian government eventually announced a resumption of palladium-mining activity, and prices dropped back to normal levels in 2001. As a result of this price shock, mining companies have tried to diversify their activities beyond Russia and South Africa. However, there's no way around the fact that most of the world's reserves of palladium ore are located in these two countries. As a matter of fact, perhaps no two countries dominate a commodity as much as Russia and South Africa dominate palladium.

Keep in mind the unique market structure as you consider investing in this precious metal.

One of the best — albeit indirect — methods of getting exposure to the palladium markets is investing in companies that mine the metal. A number of companies specialize in this activity, but I recommend taking a look at these two:

✔ **North American Palladium (AMEX: PAL):** North American Palladium, headquartered in Toronto, has a significant presence in the Canadian palladium ore–mining business. It's the largest producer of palladium in Canada. North American palladium is your entry into the lucrative Canadian palladium-mining sector.

✔ **Stillwater Mining Company (NYSE: SWC):** Stillwater Mining, based in Montana, is the largest producer of palladium outside South Africa and Russia. Although it's involved in platinum and other PGM, its primary mining output is palladium. It produces approximately 500,000 ounces of palladium a year, primarily through North American mines.

Although these are the two largest companies that trade publicly on American exchanges, several international companies have significantly larger palladium-mining activities. Just make sure you're aware of the many regulatory differences between American and overseas markets before you invest in companies that trade in overseas stock markets.

You may also want to consider a couple international palladium companies:

✔ **Anglo Platinum Group (South Africa):** As its name suggests, Anglo Platinum Group invests in platinum group metals, but it's also one of the largest producers of palladium in the world. The company produced more than 2.5 million ounces of palladium in 2005 and is estimated to have reserves of more than 200 million ounces (this includes other PGM). With its operations located primarily in South Africa, Anglo Platinum Group is your gateway to South African palladium. Its shares are traded in the Johannesburg Stock Exchange (JSE) and the London Stock Exchange (LSE).

✔ **Norilsk Nickel (Russia):** Norilsk Nickel may not be a household name, but it's the largest producer of palladium in the world. It dominates the Russian palladium industry, which is the largest in the world (see Table 8-6). Beyond its large palladium-mining activities, the company is a major player in copper and nickel ore mining. The company's shares are available through the Moscow Inter-bank Currency Exchange (MICEX).

If you're comfortable in the futures markets (covered in Chapter 13), the Chicago Mercantile Exchange (CME) offers a futures contract that tracks palladium. This contract represents 100 troy ounces of palladium and trades both electronically and during the open outcry session. It trades under the symbol PA.

Zinc and Grow Rich

Zinc is the fourth most widely used metal, right behind iron/steel, aluminum, and copper. Zinc has unique abilities to resist corrosion and oxidation and is used for metal *galvanization,* the process of applying a metal coating to another metal to prevent rust and corrosion. As you can see from Table 8-7, galvanizing metals (particularly steel) is by far the largest application of zinc.

Table 8-7	Zinc Consumption by Sector
Sector	*% of Market Consumption*
Galvanization	47
Brass and bronze coatings	19
Zinc alloying	15
Other	14

Source: London Metal Exchange

The best way to invest in zinc is to go through the futures markets. The London Metal Exchange (LME) offers a futures contract for zinc that has been trading since the early 1900s and is the industry benchmark for zinc pricing. The contract trades in lots of 25 tons and is available for trading during the current month and the subsequent 27 months.

You Won't Get Nickel and Dimed by Investing in Nickel

Nickel is a *ferrous metal,* which means it belongs to the iron group of metals. It's an important industrial metal that's used as an alloy with metals such as iron and copper, and it's sought after because of its ductility, malleability, and resistance to corrosion.

One of nickel's primary applications is in creating stainless steel. When steel is alloyed with nickel, its resistance to corrosion increases dramatically. Because stainless steel is a necessity of modern life, and a large portion of nickel goes toward creating this important metal alloy, you can rest assured that demand for nickel will remain strong. As you can see from Table 8-8, although nickel has many important uses, the creation of stainless steel remains its primary application.

Table 8-8   Nickel Consumption by Sector

Sector	% of Market Consumption
Stainless steel	65
Nonferrous alloys	12
Ferrous alloys	10
Electroplating	8
Other	5

Source: London Metal Exchange

Australia has the largest reserves of nickel, and its proximity to the rapidly industrializing Asian center — China and India — is a strategic advantage. Another major player in the nickel markets is Russia; the Russian company Norilsk Nickel (covered in the section on palladium earlier in this chapter) is the largest producer of nickel in the world. Nickel mining is a labor-intensive industry, but countries that have large reserves of this special metal are poised to do very well. Check out the countries with the largest reserves of nickel in Table 8-9.

Table 8-9   Largest Nickel Reserves, 2015

Country	% of Total
Australia	37
Russia	14
Indonesia	12
New Caledonia	8
Canada	5

(continued)

Table 8-9 (continued)

Country	% of Total
Cuba	3
Philippines	2.5
Papua New Guinea	2
Brazil	2
China	1.5

Source: U.S. Geological Survey

The LME offers a futures contract for nickel. The nickel futures contract on the LME gives you the most direct access to the nickel market. It trades in lots of 6 tons, and its tick size is $5 per ton. As with zinc, it trades during the first month, as well as 27 subsequent months.

The term *nickel,* used to denote the 5-cent coin, is misleading because the coin actually consists primarily of copper (75 percent). Nickel, the metal, makes up only 25 percent of nickel, the coin.

Chapter 9

Unearthing the Potential: Investing in Mining Companies

* *

In This Chapter

▶ Understanding mining companies and their investment suitability

▶ Examining specialized mining companies

▶ Identifying the mining conglomerates

* *

*T*rading metals outright — through the futures markets — can be tricky for the uninitiated trader. You have to keep track of a number of moving pieces, such as contract expiration dates, margin calls, trading months, and other variables. In addition, metals on the futures markets can be subject to extreme price volatility, and you can set yourself up for disastrous losses. So it's understandable if you don't want to trade metals futures contracts. But this doesn't mean that you should ignore the whole metals subasset class altogether, because you may miss out on some substantial returns.

One possible avenue for opening up your portfolio to metals is to invest in companies that specialize in mining metals and minerals. A number of such companies exist, and their performance has been stellar in recent years. For example, Rio Tinto (NYSE: RTP), a mining conglomerate that I discuss in this chapter, saw its stock price surge over 100 percent in the mid-2000s era. Although not all mining companies have had similar performances, ignoring such a large group of the market is not advisable.

In this chapter, I look at the top mining companies — both the conglomerates and the specialized ones — to help you identify the best ones to include in your portfolio.

I provide you only a snapshot of recent financial performance here. Before you invest in any company, you should look at a number of metrics to determine its financial health. Go through the balance sheet, income statement, and statement of cash flows — among other key financial statements — with a fine-toothed comb. Only if you determine that the company has a clean financial bill of health and is poised for growth should you proceed with your investment. Turn to Chapter 14 for more on the due diligence process.

Considering Diversified Mining Companies

Like the large integrated energy companies — ExxonMobil and BP, covered in Chapter 3 — diversified mining companies are involved in *all* aspects of the metals production process. These companies, which often employ tens of thousands of people, have operations in all four corners of the globe. They're involved in excavating metals — both *precious* and *base* metals, *ferrous* and *nonferrous* — as well as transforming these metals into finished products and subsequently distributing the end products to consumers.

Investing in one of these companies gives you exposure not only to a wide variety of metals, but also to the whole mining supply chain. I've selected the "best of breeds," and I evaluate their investment suitability in the following sections.

BHP Billiton

BHP Billiton is one of the largest mining companies in the world. It formed as a result of the 2001 merger between Broken Hill Proprietary, an Australian company, and Billiton, an Anglo-Dutch company. BHP Billiton, headquartered in Melbourne, Australia, has mining operations in more than 25 countries, including Australia, Canada, the United States, South Africa, and Papua New Guinea. The company processes a large number of metals, including aluminum, copper, silver, and iron; it also has small oil and natural gas operations in Algeria and Pakistan. The company is listed on the New York Stock Exchange (NYSE) under the symbol BHP.

One of the reasons I like BHP Billiton is that it offers economies of scale, meaning large-scale exposure to various sectors of the supply chain, which enhances its pricing capabilities. This is a large company, by any standard. Here's a snapshot of the company's financial performance. (All figures are for 2015.)

- ✔ **Revenues:** $96.5 billion
- ✔ **Net income:** $9.7 billion
- ✔ **Free cash flow:** $23.3 billion
- ✔ **Profit margins:** 21.4 percent

The company has benefited handsomely from the increasing prices of commodities such as copper and aluminum. As a result, BHP Billiton has been operating on a historical profit margin in the neighborhood of 20 percent.

Remember that past results don't guarantee future performance. Commodity prices are cyclical in nature, and prices for metals such as copper, silver, and aluminum can't go up in a straight line forever. Make sure that you take into account the cyclicality factor as you move forward with your commodity investments. As evidence, consider the Global Financial Crisis of 2008 and the subsequent effect it had on global equities, including BHP.

Rio Tinto

Rio Tinto is a mining company rich in both minerals and history. The Rothschild banking family founded the company in 1873 to mine ore deposits in Spain. Today Rio Tinto boasts operations in Africa, Australia, Europe, the Pacific Rim, North America, Australia, and South America. A true mining conglomerate, it's involved in all facets of the mining supply chain, from extraction to transformation and distribution.

The company is involved in the production of a number of commodities, including iron ore, copper, aluminum, and titanium. In addition, Rio Tinto has interests in diamonds, manufacturing almost 30 percent of global natural diamonds, processed primarily through its mining activities in Australia.

By investing in Rio Tinto, you get not only a company that has extensive operations across the mining complex, but also one that's in a solid financial position. Check out some numbers the company posted in 2015:

- ✔ **Revenues:** $54.6 billion
- ✔ **Net income:** $4.5 billion
- ✔ **Free cash flow:** $4.2 billion
- ✔ **Profit margins:** 11.5 percent

These strong numbers, which reflect increased demand for the commodities the company is involved in, have had a positive mid- to long-term impact on the company's stock. Rio Tinto trades on the NYSE under the ticker symbol RTP.

Anglo-American

Anglo-American PLC began mining gold in South Africa in 1917. It was a venture by British and American entrepreneurs (hence the name) who saw an opportunity in developing South African mines. Ever since, it has played an important role in the development of South Africa's gold-mining industry. Today Anglo-American has operations in all four corners of the globe and operates in more than 20 countries. It's involved in producing and distributing a wide array of metals, minerals, and natural resources, including gold, silver, and platinum, but also diamonds and paper packaging (it owns 45 percent of DeBeers, the diamond company).

I recommend Anglo-American as a long-term investment because it has been in the business for almost a century, it's involved in almost all aspects of the mining industry, and the scale of its operations is global. The company is listed in the London Stock Exchange under the ticker symbol AAL. In addition, it has American Depository Receipts listed in the NASDAQ National Market that trade under the symbol AAUK.

When a foreign company wants to access the American capital markets, it has the option of issuing its shares as *American Depository Receipts* (ADRs). A domestic bank (such as the Bank of New York, which is the largest issuer of ADRs) issues ADRs to the American investing public, while the bank holds shares of the foreign company overseas. The advantage of the ADR is that it allows American investors to invest in foreign companies without going through foreign exchanges. The ADRs trade in such a way that they reflect the daily price movements of the underlying stock as it is traded in a stock exchange overseas. For more information, you can check out the Bank of New York's Web site on ADRs, at www.adrbny.com.

Checking Out Specialized Mining Companies

The benefit of investing in diversified mining companies, like those profiled in the previous section, is that you get to "buy the market" in one fell swoop. However, what if you spot a rally in gold, copper, or another individual metal and want to profit from this specific trend? In this case, the most direct exposure through the equity markets comes by investing in companies that specialize in specific metals. I identify and evaluate some of these companies in this section.

Newmont Mining: Gold

Newmont is headquartered in Colorado but operates gold mines all over the world. It's the largest producer of gold in South America, one of the most important gold regions, and has wholly owned subsidiaries or joint ventures in Australia, Canada, and Uzbekistan.

I recommend Newmont because it's a premier player in the competitive gold-mining industry. It has some competitive advantages, including its control of 50,000 square miles of land containing more than 90 million equity ounces of gold. (*Equity ounces* is the amount of gold measured in troy ounces multiplied by the current market price of gold as measured in U.S. dollars.) In addition, it has a strong balance sheet and is in solid financial condition. Check out some of Newmont's numbers (2015 figures):

- ✔ **Revenues:** $12.5 billion
- ✔ **Net income:** $78.4 million
- ✔ **Free cash flow:** $2.5 million
- ✔ **Profit margins:** 19 percent

If you're looking for a well-managed company with extensive experience and operations in the gold-mining industry, you can't go wrong with Newmont. (Be sure to read Chapter 7 for in-depth coverage of the gold industry.)

Silver Wheaton: Silver

Silver Wheaton focuses on one thing only: silver. Some mining companies have small operations in secondary metals, but Silver Wheaton generates 100 percent of its revenues from silver mining. The company operates mines primarily in Mexico and Sweden. Its modus operandi is to purchase silver directly from the mines and sell it on the open market for a profit. As a result, the company has very little, if any, operating overhead. This results in strong revenues and cash flows, as you can see from 2015 operations:

- ✔ **Revenues:** $585 million
- ✔ **Net income:** $169 million
- ✔ **Operating cash flow:** $155 million
- ✔ **Profit margins:** 52 percent

Silver Wheaton may not generate the same kinds of revenues as Anglo-American or other large mining conglomerates, but it's a well-run company with high profit margins and stable revenues.

Silver Wheaton's numbers reflect a strong operating background. It's actually the second-largest producer of silver, in terms of annual output measured in troy ounces. It produced more than 15 million troy ounces in 2005.

For more information on the silver industry, including the top producers, the largest-consuming segments, and an analysis of additional investment methodologies, turn to Chapter 7.

Freeport McMoRan: Copper

Freeport McMoRan (NYSE: FCX) is the largest independent copper producer in the world and also has significant operations in gold mining. Freeport started operations in Texas and rapidly expanded to include other locations in the continental

United States and, later, internationally; the company has a strong footprint in Asia. In 2007, Freeport acquired its main rival, Phelps Dodge.

Phelps Dodge had quite a history in the mining industry, having been in the copper business for more than 150 years. As a mining concern, it played a key role in the industrialization of the United States. Copper was in demand by the growing nation, and Phelps Dodge supplied it. The Phelps Dodge acquisition was a huge coup for Freeport, and today the combined company is the market leader in copper production, with significant operations in the production of molybdenum and molybdenum-based chemicals.

Molybdenum (pronounced mah-*lib*-den-um) is known as a transition metal because it's principally used as an alloy with a number of metals. It has wide applications in industry — for instance, it's used in the construction of oil pipelines, aircraft engines, and missiles.

Freeport is also known for operating the largest copper mine ever discovered, the Grasberg mine in Indonesia; the proceeds from Grasberg are so prolific that Freeport is the largest individual taxpayer to the Indonesian government. Freeport is large by any standards, as evidenced by its 2015 financial performance:

- ✔ **Revenues:** $17 billion
- ✔ **Net income:** $4.7 billion
- ✔ **Operating cash flow:** $3.8 billion
- ✔ **Profit margins:** 16 percent

Overall, Freeport's performance has been positive over the last five years, although not without turbulence, due to the global financial downturn.

Phelps Dodge has an active hedging program, in which it enters into agreements with other market participants through the futures markets, to hedge against price risk. However, not all hedgers are created equal, and Phelps Dodge has taken some hits in the past as a result of its hedging activities. During the second quarter of 2006, for instance, the company's net income fell to $471.1 million from $682.3 million the previous year-over-year quarter. This was a direct result of losses it incurred in hedging-related activity. So even though the price of copper was robust during this period, and the company would have benefited from these strong prices, its external activities were negatively affected. Always make sure that you know what's going on with a company before you invest in it.

You can find more information about the copper market and industry in Chapter 8.

Alcoa: Aluminum

Alcoa is a household name, and for good reason: It's the largest producer of aluminum, which is the most ubiquitous metal in the modern world. Cars, soda cans, and fighter jets are all partly made from aluminum, and Alcoa is the primary supplier of this metal in the market today. Alcoa (an acronym that stands for Aluminum Company of America) is involved in all phases of the aluminum supply chain. It provides aluminum-based products to a wide range of customers, including the aerospace and automotive industries, individual and commercial enterprises, the manufacturing sector, and the military.

Another reason I like Alcoa is that it's making some aggressive moves overseas and signing strategic, long-term pacts with some of the top aluminum producers. It recently entered into a partnership with the Aluminum Corporation of China (NYSE: ACH), China's largest aluminum producer, and is positioning itself to capitalize on the Chinese market, possibly the largest aluminum market in the future. Alcoa has undergone some strategic changes and made some strategic acquisitions — such as purchasing its main competitor, Alcan — that have acted as a drag on its financial performance in the short term. Capturing these market synergies and experiencing some weakness in the aluminum market short term have pressured its profitability. That said, I believe these circumstances present a good opportunity to buy a solid company at a discount:

- ✔ **Revenues:** $22 billion
- ✔ **Net income:** $2.5 billion
- ✔ **Free cash flow:** $350 million
- ✔ **Profit margins:** 10 percent

The stock's performance has been choppy in recent years, so make sure that you research the company as much as possible before you take the plunge.

Be sure to read Chapter 8 for a close examination of the aluminum market.

Arcelor-Mittal: Steel

Mittal Steel, under the management of Indian-born steel magnate Lakshmi Mittal, launched an unsolicited bid to acquire Arcelor, the Luxembourg-based high-end steel manufacturer, in January 2006. After a five-month takeover battle, which involved *poison pill* and *white knight* takeover defense strategies, the boards of both companies agreed to a merger of equals. The combined entity created one of the largest independent steel companies in the world.

In mergers and acquisitions (M&A), companies fend off hostile takeovers. One of the most popular defense strategies includes pursuing a merger or acquisition with a "friendly" company, known as a white knight. Another strategy, the poison pill strategy, takes a different approach. This option involves making the company unattractive to an acquirer, such as by increasing levels of debt or increasing the number of shares outstanding to dilute their value.

The new company combines the number one and number two steel producers in the world and controls more than 10 percent of global steel output. Arcelor-Mittal is a truly global steel manufacturer, with operations in all four corners of the globe and across all stages of the steel-making process.

Turn to Chapter 8 for an in-depth examination of the global steel industry.

Making Money during the Mining Merger Mania

Profiting from the merger activity in the mining industry can be a good investment strategy. Since the year 2000, a number of large companies have entered into merger agreements (the marriage of the Australian BHP and the British Billiton, which resulted in BHP Billiton, is a good example), and this trend is likely to continue as mining companies seek to add new capacity by merging or acquiring smaller rivals.

Due to the sustained levels of high commodity prices, mining companies have large cash reserves and are looking to spend them to beef up their operations. Mergers and acquisitions present long-term value opportunities to these companies and their shareholders, and are likely to continue in the years to come. During the writing of this book, for example, Phelps Dodge (one of the largest copper-mining companies) launched a simultaneous double bid to acquire Inco and Falconbridge, both independent Canadian mining companies, in a synchronized transaction valued at more than $40 billion.

The caveat of profiting from merger announcements, of course, is identifying the "hunter" and the "hunted," the acquirer and the target. Doing so isn't easy; theoretically, any given sector has an infinite number of merger and acquisition combinations. The best plan is to regularly monitor the industry for news, special announcements, or unusual trading activity. Specifically, keep your eye out for any announcements by companies in Forms 8K (filings with the SEC that announce special situations); read news stories about the companies in the industry (I recommend reading *The Wall Street Journal's* "Heard on the Street" column); and remain alert to any sudden and unusual movements in the companies' stock activity.

Identifying possible merger announcements isn't an exact science, but it can yield some phenomenal returns. A lot of folks try to profit from insider information regarding merger deals, which is illegal and has led to some huge financial scandals. If you trade on information that's not public, you could end up going to jail — don't do it! Also remember that, as a general rule, you want to buy the "hunted" before any merger announcements because the stock price of a target company tends to increase with any merger announcement, while that of the acquiring company decreases. The logic here is that the acquiring company is paying a premium for its acquisition and will have to bear the costs of incorporating this new entity within its corporate and operational structure.

Chapter 10

Trading Agricultural Products

● ●

In This Chapter

▶ Recognizing the value of soft commodities: coffee, cocoa, sugar, and orange juice

▶ Exploring the ag commodities: corn, wheat, and soybeans

▶ Identifying opportunities in cattle, hogs, and pork bellies

● ●

*T*he commodities that kick off this chapter — coffee, cocoa, sugar, and frozen concentrated orange juice — are known as *soft commodities.* Soft commodities are commodities that are usually grown, as opposed to those that are mined (such as metals) or those that are raised (such as livestock). The *softs,* as they're sometimes known, represent a significant portion of the commodities markets. They're indispensable and cyclical, just like energy and metals, but they're also unique because they're edible and seasonal. *Seasonality* is a major distinguishing characteristic of soft commodities because they can be grown only during specific times of the year and in specific geographical locations — usually in tropical areas. (This is why these commodities are also known as *tropical commodities.*)

I also look at some of the major agricultural commodities that trade in the futures markets. These commodities, sometimes simply known as *ags,* are a unique component of the broader commodities markets. They're labor intensive and subject to volatility because of underlying market fundamentals; however, they also present solid investment opportunities.

Livestock, like the tropical and grain commodities, is a unique category in the agricultural commodities subasset class. It's not a widely followed area of the commodities markets — unlike crude oil, for example, you're not likely to see feeder cattle prices quoted on the nightly news — but this doesn't mean that you can ignore this area of the markets.

That said, raising livestock is a time-consuming and labor-intensive undertaking, and the markets are susceptible and sensitive to minor disruption. These contracts are volatile, so venture into this area of the market only if you have an iron-clad grasp on the concepts behind futures trading — along with a high tolerance for risk.

This chapter analyzes the markets for these challenging but essential commodities.

Giving Your Portfolio a Buzz by Investing in Coffee

Coffee, which originated in Arabia sometime in the 15th century, is today the second most widely traded commodity in terms of physical volume — behind only crude oil.

As with a number of other commodities, coffee production is dominated by a handful of countries. Brazil has historically been the top producer of coffee in the world and has held this position for several decades. Traditionally, Colombia has held the number two spot, but it's lost that position to up-and-comers such as Vietnam and Indonesia. Table 10-1 lists the largest coffee-producing countries.

Table 10-1	Top Coffee Producers, 2015
Country	*Production (Thousands of Bags)*
Brazil	39,470
Vietnam	18,000
Indonesia	11,380
Colombia	8,500

Country	Production (Thousands of Bags)
India	4,827
Ethiopia	4,500
Mexico	4,200
Honduras	3,527
Guatemala	3,500
Uganda	3,000

Source: International Coffee Organization

Large-scale coffee production is measured in *bags*. One bag of coffee weighs 60 kilograms, or approximately 132 pounds.

If you want to further investigate the ins and outs of the coffee markets, I recommend you visit these websites for more information:

✔ **International Coffee Organization:** www.ico.org

✔ **National Coffee Association of the USA:** www.ncausa.org

Just as choosing the right flavor is important when buying your cup of coffee, knowing the different types of coffees available for investment is crucial. The world's coffee production is pretty much made up of two types of beans:

✔ **Arabica:** Arabica coffee is the most widely grown coffee plant in the world, accounting for more than 60 percent of global coffee production. Arabica is grown in countries as diverse as Brazil and Indonesia. It's the premium coffee bean, adding a richer taste to any brew, and, as a result, is the most expensive coffee bean in the world. Because of its high quality, it serves as the benchmark for coffee prices all over the world.

✔ **Robusta:** Robusta accounts for about 40 percent of total coffee production. Because it's easier to grow than Arabica coffee, it's also less expensive.

You have several ways to invest in coffee production. One way is to buy coffee in the futures markets; the other is to invest in companies that specialize in running gourmet coffee shops.

The coffee futures contract: It may be your cup of tea

The coffee futures markets determine the future price of coffee and, more importantly, protect producers and purchasers of coffee from wild price swings. In addition to hedging opportunities, the coffee futures markets allow individual investors to profit from coffee price variations. The most liquid coffee futures contract is available on the Intercontinental Exchange (ICE), which assumed tradability of the coffee contract when it acquired the New York Board of Trade (NYBOT).

Take a look at its contract specs:

- ✔ **Contract ticker symbol:** KC
- ✔ **Contract size:** 37,500 pounds
- ✔ **Underlying commodity:** Pure Arabica coffee
- ✔ **Price fluctuation:** $0.0005 per pound ($18.75 per contract)
- ✔ **Trading months:** March, May, July, September, and December

Because of seasonality, cyclicality, and geopolitical factors, coffee can be a volatile commodity subject to extreme price swings. Be sure to research the coffee markets inside and out before investing.

Ordering up investments in gourmet coffee shops

In New York City, where I live, as in most other metropolitan areas, you can't walk a block without spotting two or three gourmet coffee shops, especially Starbucks. Coffee shops are nothing new — Arabian coffee shops sprang up in the Middle East as early as the 15th century. Today coffee shops are still a place where you can enjoy a nice (and big) cup of joe while socializing with friends.

But behind the relaxed, laid-back atmosphere is a complex moneymaking operation. Coffee is serious business, and you can profit from the coffee craze that has gripped the United States (the largest consumer of coffee in the world) and is spreading throughout Europe and newly developing countries such as India and China: Simply invest in the companies that are capitalizing on this trend. Find out where your $4.50 for a cup of coffee is going, and profit from it.

You're probably familiar with Starbucks; a number of other gourmet coffee shops and distributors provide you with good investment opportunity as well. These purveyors of coffee include the following:

✔ **Starbucks Corp. (NASDAQ: SBUX):** Perhaps no other brand has come to represent an entire industry as Starbucks has coffee. (The only other brands that come to mind are Kleenex with tissues and Xerox with photocopiers.) Starbucks is a cultural phenomenon, but, more important, it's also a financial juggernaut. This is a $20-billion company with about $10 billion in revenue (according to 2009 figures). Starbucks dominates the entire coffee supply chain, from purchasing and roasting to selling and marketing. It has more than 10,000 stores worldwide, primarily in the United States and Europe, but also in China, Singapore, and even Saudi Arabia.

✔ **Peet's Coffee and Tea, Inc. (NASDAQ: PEET):** Peet's Coffee operates only about 100 coffee shops, but its strength lies in distribution. The company sells a large selection of coffees, produced in countries as diverse as Guatemala and Kenya, to customers across the United States, including restaurants and grocery stores.

✔ **Green Mountain Coffee Roaster, Inc. (NASDAQ: GMCR):** Green Mountain Coffee, with headquarters in Vermont, distributes specialized coffee products. It sells premium Arabica coffee to a number of entities, such as convenience stores, specialty retailers, and restaurants. It has a large presence on the East Coast and has a partnership with Paul Newman's company, Newman's Own, to provide organic coffee to customers. This company is a good one if you want exposure to the high-end coffee distribution market in the Northeast.

Warming Up to Cocoa

Cocoa is a fermented seed from the cacao tree, which is usually grown in hot and rainy regions around the equator. The first cacao tree is said to have originated in South America, where cocoa beans were used for both consumption and monetary purposes. European traders came across the cacao tree and were so impressed with the tasty beverages made from cocoa beans that they brought some back to Europe, where cocoa beans were then turned into chocolate. From Europe, the cacao tree was introduced to Africa. Today African countries dominate the cocoa trade, as you can see in Table 10-2.

Table 10-2	Top Cocoa Producers, 2015
Country	*Production (Thousands of Tons)*
Ivory Coast	1,190
Ghana	650
Indonesia	535
Nigeria	260
Cameroon	200
Brazil	155
Ecuador	150
Colombia	50
Mexico	45
Papua New Guinea	40

Source: International Cocoa Organization

Cocoa production for import and export purposes is measured in metric tons. For a more nuanced understanding of the cocoa market and the companies that control it, check out these resources:

✔ **Cocoa Producer's Alliance:** www.copal-cpa.org

✔ **International Cocoa Organization:** www.icco.org

✔ **World Cocoa Foundation:** www.worldcocoa foundation.org

The ICE offers a futures contract for cocoa. Consider some useful information regarding this cocoa futures contract, which is the most liquid in the market:

- ✔ **Contract ticker symbol:** CC
- ✔ **Contract size:** 10 metric tons
- ✔ **Underlying commodity:** Generic cocoa beans
- ✔ **Price fluctuation:** $1 per ton ($10 per contract)
- ✔ **Trading months:** March, May, July, September, and December

As with coffee, the cocoa market is subject to seasonal and cyclical factors that have a large impact on price movements. It can be pretty volatile.

Investing in Sugar: Sweet Move!

Sugar production reportedly started more than 9,000 years ago in southeastern Asia, where it was used in India and China for medicinal purposes. It then spread to southern Europe through Persia and Arabia around 400 B.C. In Europe and the Middle East, sugar became a popular food sweetener. From Europe, sugar spread to the New World in the 15th century and was particularly suitable for growing in Latin America. Today Latin American countries dominate the sugar trade; Brazil is the largest sugar producer in the world, as you can see in Table 10-3. In 2015, the top ten sugar producers accounted for 74 percent of global production.

Table 10-3	Top Sugar Producers, 2015
Country	*Production (Millions of Tons)*
Brazil	36
E.U.	18
India	17
China	13
Thailand	8
United States	7

(continued)

Table 10-3 *(continued)*

Country	Production (Millions of Tons)
South Africa	6
Mexico	5
Australia	4.5
Russia	4

Source: United States Department of Agriculture

If you're interested in investing in sugar, the ICE offers two futures contracts that track the price of sugar: Sugar #11 (world production) and sugar #14 (U.S. production). Consider the contract specs for these two sugar contracts:

✔ **Sugar #11 (World)**

- **Contract ticker symbol:** SB
- **Contract size:** 112,000 pounds
- **Underlying commodity:** Global sugar
- **Price fluctuation:** $0.01 per pound ($11.20 per contract)
- **Trading months:** March, May, July, and October

✔ **Sugar #14 (USA)**

- **Contract ticker symbol:** SE
- **Contract size:** 112,000 pounds
- **Underlying commodity:** Domestic (U.S.) sugar
- **Price fluctuation:** $0.01 per pound ($11.20 per contract)
- **Trading months:** January, March, May, July, September, and November

On a historical basis, sugar #14 produced in the United States tends to be more expensive than sugar #11. However, sugar #11 accounts for most of the volume in the ICE sugar market.

Orange Juice: Refreshingly Good for Your Bottom Line

Orange juice is one of the only actively traded contracts in the futures markets that's based on a tropical fruit: oranges. Oranges are widely grown in the Western Hemisphere, particularly in Florida and Brazil. Brazil is by far the largest producer of oranges, although the United States — primarily Florida — is also a major player.

Because oranges are perishable, the futures contract tracks *frozen concentrated orange juice* (FCOJ). This particular form is suitable for storage and fits one of the criteria for inclusion in the futures arena: that the underlying commodity be deliverable. This contract is available for trade on the ICE. The ICE includes two versions of the FCOJ contract: one that tracks the Florida/Brazil oranges and another one based on global production. Here are specs of FCOJ on the ICE:

✔ **FCOJ-A (Florida/Brazil)**

- **Contract ticker symbol:** OJ

- **Contract size:** 15,000 pounds

- **Underlying commodity:** FCOJ from Brazil and/or Florida only

- **Price fluctuation:** $0.0005 per pound ($7.50 per contract)

- **Trading months:** January, March, May, July, September, and November

✔ **FCOJ-B (World)**

- **Contract ticker symbol:** OB

- **Contract size:** 15,000 pounds

- **Underlying commodity:** FCOJ from any producing country

- **Price fluctuation:** $0.0005 per pound ($7.50 per contract)

- **Trading months:** January, March, May, July, September, and November

The production of oranges is very sensitive to weather. For instance, the hurricane season common in the Florida region can have a significant impact on the prices of oranges both on the spot market and in the futures market. Be sure to consider weather and seasonality when investing in FCOJ futures.

Field of Dreams: Investing in Corn

Approximately 35 million hectares of land are used exclusively for the production of corn worldwide, a business that the U.S. Department of Agriculture values at more than $20 billion a year. Corn is an important food source for both humans and animals and, unlike other grains, can be grown in a wide variety of climates and conditions, making it an important cash crop. Beyond feedstock, corn has other important applications and is processed into starches, corn oil, and even fuel ethanol. Corn is definitely big business.

Corn, like other commodities, such as crude oil (see Chapter 3) and coffee (earlier in this chapter), comes in different qualities. The most important types of corn to be familiar with are *high-grade number 2* and *number 3 yellow corn,* which are both traded in the futures markets.

The most direct way of investing in corn is to go through the futures markets. A corn contract, courtesy of the Chicago Mercantile Exchange (CME), helps farmers, consumers, and investors manage and profit from the underlying market opportunities. Take a look at the contract specs:

- **Contract ticker symbol (open outcry):** C
- **Electronic ticker (CME Globex):** ZC
- **Contract size:** 5,000 bushels
- **Underlying commodity:** High-grade no. 2 or no. 3 yellow corn
- **Price fluctuation:** $0.0025 per bushel ($12.50 per contract)
- **Trading hours:** 9:05 a.m. to 1:00 p.m. open outcry; 6:30 p.m. to 6:00 a.m. electronic (CST)

It's important to know the trading hours for corn and other commodities that trade both on the open outcry and through electronic trading. Open outcry hours are a legacy from the pre-Internet age, when people traded all contracts on the trading floor; you can still participate in this trading method during the hours noted in this chapter. The electronic trading system is the latest addition and is much quicker, so you can be sure to get your orders placed quickly and efficiently. As of the writing of this book, the open outcry system is slowly being phased out; eventually, electronic trading will permanently replace it.

✔ **Trading months:** March, May, July, September, and December

Corn futures contracts are usually measured in bushels (as with the corn contract the CME offers). Large-scale corn production and consumption is measured in metric tons.

Historically, the United States has dominated the corn markets — and still does, thanks to abundant land and helpful governmental subsidies. China is also a major player and exhibits potential for becoming a market leader in the future. Other notable producers include Brazil, Mexico, and India. Table 10-4 lists the top producers.

Table 10-4	Top Corn Producers, 2015
Country	*Production (Millions of Tons)*
United States	307
China	165
Brazil	51
Mexico	25
India	18.5
South Africa	12.7
Argentina	12.6
Ukraine	11.4
Canada	10.5

Source: U.S. Department of Agriculture

Similar to other agricultural commodities, corn is subject to seasonal and cyclical factors that have a direct, and often powerful, effect on prices. Prices for corn can go through roller-coaster rides, with wild swings in short periods of time.

For more information on the corn markets, check out the following sources:

- ✔ **Corn Refiners Association:** www.corn.org
- ✔ **National Corn Growers Association:** www.ncga.com
- ✔ **USDA Corn Research Service:** www.ers.usda.gov/briefing/corn

Welcome to the Bread Basket: Investing in Wheat

Wheat is the second most widely produced agricultural commodity in the world (on a per-volume basis), right behind corn and ahead of rice. World wheat production came in at 682 million metric tons in 2009, according to the U.S. Department of Agriculture (USDA).

Unlike other commodities that are dominated by single producers — Saudi Arabia and oil, for example — no single country dominates wheat production. As you can see from Table 10-5, the major wheat producers are a surprisingly eclectic group. The advanced developing countries of China and India are the two largest producers, and industrial countries like Canada and Germany also boast significant wheat-production capabilities.

Table 10-5	Top Wheat Producers, 2009
Country	*Production (Millions of Tons)*
China	115
India	81
Russia	61
United States	60
France	38

Country	Production (Millions of Tons)
Canada	26.5
Germany	25.2
Pakistan	24
Australia	21
Ukraine	21

Source: U.S. Department of Agriculture

Wheat is measured in bushels, for investment and accounting purposes. Each bushel contains approximately 60 pounds of wheat. As for most other agricultural commodities, metric tons are used to quantify total production and consumption figures on a national and international basis.

The most direct way of accessing the wheat markets, short of owning a wheat farm, is to trade the wheat futures contract. As with the other agricultural commodities discussed in this chapter, the CME offers a futures contract for those interested in capturing profits from wheat price movements — whether for hedging or speculative purposes. Here are the specs for the CME futures contract:

- ✔ **Contract ticker symbol (open outcry):** W

- ✔ **Electronic ticker (CME Globex):** ZW

- ✔ **Contract size:** 5,000 bushels

- ✔ **Underlying commodity:** Premium wheat

- ✔ **Price fluctuation:** $0.0025 per bushel ($12.50 per contract)

- ✔ **Trading hours:** 9:30 a.m. to 1:15 p.m. open outcry; 6:32 p.m. to 6:00 a.m. electronic (CST)

- ✔ **Trading months:** March, May, July, September, and December

Wheat production, like that of corn and soybeans, is a seasonal enterprise that's subject to various output disruptions. For instance, Kazakhstan, an important producer, has faced issues with wheat production in the past related to underinvestment in machinery and the misuse of fertilizers. This mismanagement of resources has an impact on the acreage yield, which then impacts prices. Such disruptions on the supply side can have a magnified effect on futures prices.

The following sources have more info on the wheat market:

- ✔ **National Association of Wheat Growers:** www. wheatworld.org

- ✔ **U.S. Wheat Associates:** www.uswheat.org

- ✔ **Wheat Foods Council:** www.wheatfoods.org

Many organizations that offer information on specific commodities, such as corn and wheat, are specialized lobby groups whose agenda — alongside providing information to the public — includes promoting the consumption of the products they represent. Keep this in mind as you research.

It's Not Just Peanuts: Trading Soybeans

Soybeans have been cultivated for centuries, starting in Asia. Soybeans are a vital crop for the world economy, used in everything from producing poultry feedstock to creating vegetable oil. In this section, I introduce you to the different soybean extracts you can trade: soybeans, soybean oil, and soybean meal.

Check out the following reputable resources:

- ✔ **American Soybean Association:** www.soygrowers.org

- ✔ **Iowa Soybean Association:** www.iasoybeans.com

- ✔ **Soy Protein Council:** www.spcouncil.org

- ✔ **Soy Stat Reference Guide:** www.soystats.com

Soybeans

Although most soybeans are used to extract soybean oil (used as vegetable oil for culinary purposes) and soybean meal (used primarily as an agricultural feedstock), whole soybeans are also a tradable commodity.

The United States dominates the soybean market, accounting for more than 50 percent of total global production. Brazil is a distant second, with about 20 percent of the market. The crop in the United States begins in September, and soybean production is cyclical.

The most direct way to trade soybeans is through the CME soybean futures contract. Here's the contract information:

- ✔ **Contract ticker symbol (open outcry):** S
- ✔ **Electronic ticker (CME Globex):** ZS
- ✔ **Contract size:** 5,000 bushels
- ✔ **Underlying commodity:** Premium no. 1, no. 2, and no. 3 yellow soybean bushels
- ✔ **Price fluctuation:** $0.0025 per bushel ($12.50 per contract)
- ✔ **Trading hours:** 9:30 a.m. to 1:15 p.m. open outcry; 6:31 p.m. to 6:00 a.m. electronic (CST)
- ✔ **Trading months:** January, March, May, July, August, September, and November

Soybean oil

You and I know it as vegetable oil, the most widely used culinary oil in the world, partly because of its healthy, nutritional characteristics. It contains about 85 percent unsaturated fat and very little saturated fat.

In addition to its gastronomic uses, soybean oil is becoming an increasingly popular additive in alternative energy sources technology, such as biodiesel. For example, an increasing number of cars in the United States and abroad are being outfitted with engines that allow them to convert from regular diesel to soybean oil during operation. Because of their economic fuel mileage and low environmental impact, these soybean oil–enabled cars, known as *frybrids,* are becoming more popular.

Demand for soybean oil has increased in recent years as demand for these cleaner-burning fuels increases and as the automotive technology becomes better able to accommodate the usage of such biodiesels. If you want to trade soybean oil, you need to go through the CME, which offers the standard soybean oil contract. Here's the contract information:

- ✔ **Contract ticker symbol (open outcry):** BO
- ✔ **Electronic ticker (CME Globex):** ZL
- ✔ **Contract size:** 60,000 pounds
- ✔ **Underlying commodity:** Premium crude soybean oil

✔ **Price fluctuation:** $0.0001 per pound ($6 per contract)

✔ **Trading hours:** 9:30 a.m. to 1:15 p.m. open outcry;
6:31 p.m. to 6:00 a.m. electronic (CST)

✔ **Trading months:** January, March, May, July, August,
September, October, and December

For more information on investing in soybean oil, turn to the
National Oilseed Processors Association at www.nopa.org.

Soybean meal

Soybean meal, like soybean oil, is an extract of soybeans.
Basically, whatever is left after soybean oil is extracted from
soybeans can be converted to soybean meal. Soybean meal is
a high-protein, high-energy-content food used primarily as a
feedstock for cattle, hogs, and poultry.

To invest in soybean meal, you can trade the soybean meal
futures contract on the CME. Here's the information to help
you get started trading this contract:

✔ **Contract ticker symbol (open outcry):** SM

✔ **Electronic ticker (CME Globex):** ZM

✔ **Contract size:** 100 tons

✔ **Underlying commodity:** 48% protein soybean meal

✔ **Price fluctuation:** $0.10 per ton ($10 per contract)

✔ **Trading hours:** 9:30 a.m. to 1:15 p.m. open outcry;
6:31 p.m. to 6:00 a.m. electronic (CST)

✔ **Trading months:** January, March, May, July, August,
September, October, and December

You can get more information regarding soybean meal from
the Soybean Meal Information Center, at www.soymeal.org.

Holy Cow! Investing in Cattle

Cows are a special breed because they're low-maintenance
animals with high product output: They eat almost nothing
but grass, yet they produce milk, provide meat, and, in some

cases, create leather goods. This input-to-output ratio means that cows occupy a special place in the agricultural complex.

Two futures contracts exist for the cattle trader and investor: the live cattle and the feeder cattle contracts. Both trade on the Chicago Mercantile Exchange (CME).

Live cattle

The live cattle futures contract, traded on the CME, is unique because it was the first contract the CME launched to track a commodity that's actually alive. Before the live cattle futures, all futures contracts were for storable commodities, such as crude oil, copper, and sugar. The CME live cattle futures contract, launched in 1964, heralded a new era for the exchanges. Various market players, including cattle producers, packers, consumers, and independent traders, now widely trade this futures contract.

Consider the specs of this futures contract:

- **Contract ticker symbol (open outcry):** LC
- **Electronic ticker (CME Globex):** LE
- **Contract size:** 40,000 pounds
- **Underlying commodity:** Live cattle (55% choice, 45% select, Yield Grade 3 live steers)
- **Price fluctuation:** $0.00025 per pound ($10 per contract)
- **Trading hours:** 9:05 a.m. to 1:00 p.m. (CST), electronic and open outcry
- **Trading months:** February, April, June, August, October, and December

The live cattle contract is popular partly because it allows all interested parties to hedge their market positions, to reduce the volatility and uncertainty associated with livestock production in general and live cattle growing in particular.

If you decide to trade this contract, keep the following market risks in mind: seasonality, fluctuating prices of feedstock, transportation costs, changing consumer demand, and threat of diseases (such as mad cow disease). The market for the live cattle contract can be fairly volatile.

Feeder cattle

The CME launched a feeder cattle futures contract in 1971, only a few years after the launch of the groundbreaking live cattle contract. The feeder cattle contract is for calves that weigh in at 650–849 pounds, which are sent to the feedlots to get fed, fattened, and then slaughtered.

Because the CME feeder cattle futures contract is settled on a cash basis, the CME calculates an index for feeder cattle cash prices based on a seven-day average. This index, known in the industry as the *CME Feeder Cattle Index,* is an average of feeder cattle prices from the largest feeder cattle–producing states in the United States, as compiled by the U.S. Department of Agriculture (USDA). You can get information on the CME Feeder Cattle Index at www.cme.com.

To get livestock statistical information, check out the U.S. Department of Agriculture's statistical division, at www.marketnews.usda.gov/portal/lg.

Look over the specs of this futures contract:

- ✔ **Contract ticker symbol (open outcry):** FC

- ✔ **Electronic ticker (CME Globex):** GF

- ✔ **Contract size:** 50,000 pounds

- ✔ **Underlying commodity:** Feeder cattle (650–849 pound steers, medium-large #1 and medium-large #1–2)

- ✔ **Price fluctuation:** $0.00025 per pound ($12.50 per contract)

- ✔ **Trading hours:** 9:05 a.m. to 1:00 p.m. (CST), electronic and open outcry

- ✔ **Trading months:** January, March, April, May, August, September, October, and November

Lean and Mean: Checking Out Lean Hogs

The lean hog futures contract (which is a contract for the hog's carcass) trades on the CME and is used primarily by producers of lean hogs — both domestic and international — and pork importers/exporters. Launched in 1997, the lean hog contract is a fairly new addition to the CME, intended to replace the live hog futures contract that was retired. The lean hog contract replaced the live hog contract because producers and consumers of these products don't transact the live animal (live hog); it made more sense for the futures contract to track the product traded in the marketplace.

Here are the contract specs for lean hogs:

- ✔ **Contract ticker symbol (open outcry):** LH
- ✔ **Electronic ticker (CME Globex):** HE
- ✔ **Contract size:** 40,000 pounds
- ✔ **Underlying commodity:** Lean hogs (hog barrow and gilt carcasses)
- ✔ **Price fluctuation:** $0.00025 per pound ($10 per contract)
- ✔ **Trading hours:** 9:10 a.m. to 1:00 p.m. (CST), electronic and open outcry
- ✔ **Trading months:** February, April, May, June, July, August, October, and December

Perhaps no other commodity, agricultural or otherwise, exhibits the same level of volatility as the lean hogs futures contract. One of the reasons is that, compared to other products, this contract isn't very liquid: It's primarily used by commercial entities seeking to hedge against price risk. Other commodities that are actively traded by individual speculators as well as the commercial entities (such as crude oil) are far more liquid and, therefore, less volatile. If you're intent on trading this contract, know that you're up against some large and very experienced players in this market.

You Want Bacon with That? Trading Frozen Pork Bellies

Essentially, the term *pork bellies* is the traders' way of referring to bacon. Physically, pork bellies come from the underside of a hog and weigh approximately 12 pounds. These pork bellies are generally stored frozen for extended periods of time, pending delivery to consumers.

As with most other livestock products, the CME offers a futures contract for frozen pork bellies. This contract, launched by the CME in 1961, is the first-ever contract on a commodity exchange for which the underlying deliverable commodity is a meat — albeit, dead meat. (The CME live cattle contract was the first based on a live animal; refer to that section earlier in this chapter for more information.)

Here are the specs for frozen pork bellies contracts:

- ✔ **Contract ticker symbol (open outcry):** PB
- ✔ **Electronic ticker (CME Globex):** GPB
- ✔ **Contract size:** 40,000 pounds
- ✔ **Underlying commodity:** Pork bellies, cut and trimmed (12- to 18-pound frozen pork bellies)
- ✔ **Price fluctuation:** $0.00025 per pound ($10 per contract)
- ✔ **Trading hours:** 9:10 a.m. to 1:00 p.m. (CST), electronic and open outcry
- ✔ **Trading months:** February, March, May, July, and August

The pork bellies market is a seasonal market subject to wild price fluctuations. Although production of pork bellies is a major determining factor of market prices, other variables have a significant impact on prices. A buildup in pork belly inventories usually takes place at the beginning of the calendar year, resulting in lower prices. But as inventories are depleted, the market moves to a supply-side bias, placing upward pressure on market prices. On the other side of the equation, consumer demand for bacon and other meats isn't easily predictable and fluctuates with the seasons.

Because of the cyclicality of the supply-side model, coupled with the seasonality of the demand model, pork belly prices are subject to extreme volatility. As a matter of fact, the pork bellies futures contract is one of the most volatile contracts trading in the market today. Demand for bacon and other high-fat, high-cholesterol foods appears to be waning as a result of the health-conscious eating trends.

Part IV

Selecting an Investment Approach

Three Steps for Creating a Financial Road Map

- ✔ **Calculate your net worth:** Your net worth determines how much you can allocate to investments, living expenses, and retirement. You calculate it by subtracting your total liabilities from your total assets.

- ✔ **Identify your tax bracket:** Taxes impact how much of your assets you get to keep and can put a dent in your portfolio. How much you pay in taxes is based on your tax bracket.

- ✔ **Determine your appetite for risk:** Risk is perhaps the greatest enemy you face as an investor. You have to find out how to manage, tame, and minimize risk.

Find out how to make money using an index at www. dummies.com/extras/investingincommodities.

In this part . . .

- ✔ Create your financial road map and design a portfolio that includes commodities

- ✔ Check out ETFs, their pros and cons, how to choose a suitable product, and how to choose and invest in indexes

- ✔ Navigate futures contracts, trade on margin, spot market movements, and disentangle options contracts

- ✔ Invest in mutual funds, check out about master limited partnerships, work with commodity trading advisors and commodity pools, and trade on commodity exchanges

Chapter 11

Welcoming Commodities into Your Portfolio

● ●

In This Chapter

▶ Creating a financial road map

▶ Designing a portfolio that includes commodities

▶ Identifying the best ways to invest in commodities

● ●

*W*hether you're an experienced investor or a first-time trader, it's important to have a good grasp on how to use your portfolio to improve your overall financial situation. When designing your portfolio, you need to consider factors such as your risk tolerance, tax bracket, and level of liabilities. I start off this chapter by going through these basic portfolio-management techniques so that you can synchronize your portfolio with your personal financial profile.

In the second half of the chapter, I show you how to introduce commodities into your portfolio. I go through basic portfolio-allocation methods and include an overview of the benefits of diversification. In the last part of the chapter, I list the different investment methods you have at your disposal to get exposure to commodities, from index funds to master limited partnerships.

If you've ever wondered how to actually include commodities in your portfolio, you can't afford to skip this chapter!

The Color of Money: Taking Control of Your Financial Life

You invest because you've realized that it's better to have your money working for you than to have it sit in a bank account earning so little interest that you end up losing money when you factor in inflation. Most people end up working for their money all their lives, and they get stuck in a vicious cycle where they become servants to money.

If you're caught in this vicious cycle, you want your relationship with money to do a 180-degree reversal: Instead of working hard for your money, you need to have your money work hard for you! Investing allows you to build and, more important, maintain your wealth. (In the following sections, I show you how to use commodities to achieve this goal.)

Building wealth isn't easy, but with a little discipline and self-control, it can be a fun and rewarding process. If you're new to investing in general, check out Eric Tyson's *Personal Finance For Dummies* and *Investing For Dummies* (Wiley) for foundational information and guidance.

Often the accumulation phase isn't the biggest challenge to building wealth; many times being able to preserve wealth is more difficult. Keep in mind these factors that can negatively impact your bottom line:

✔ **Inflation:** *Inflation,* an increase in prices or the money supply, which can result in a quick deterioration of value, is one of the most detrimental forces you face as an investor. Inflation keeps some of the brightest minds up at night; among them is the Chairman of the Federal Reserve, whose main priority is making sure that the economy doesn't grow so fast that it creates bad inflation. When inflation gets out of control, the currency literally isn't worth the paper it's printed on. This state, known as *hyperinflation,* occurred in Weimar Germany in the 1920s. At its worst, people placed paper money in their stoves to heat themselves during the winter because the money burned longer than wood. Conveniently, one way to protect yourself from inflation is to invest in commodities such as gold and silver. (Chapter 7 has more on using precious metals as a hedge against inflation.)

✔ **Business cycles:** In the world of investing, nothing ever goes up in a straight line. Minor turbulence always arises along the way, and most investments usually experience some drops before they reach new highs — that is, if they ever reach new highs! The economy moves in the same way, alternating between expansions and recessions. Certain assets that perform well during expansions (such as stocks) don't do so well during recessions. Alternatively, assets such as commodities do fairly well during late expansionary and early recessionary phases of the business cycle. As an investor interested in preserving and growing your capital base, you need to be able to identify and invest in assets that are going to perform and generate returns, regardless of the current business cycle. I discuss the performance of commodities across the business cycle in Chapter 2.

You can minimize these risks and others, such as risks posed by fraud, the markets, and geopolitics, with some due diligence and a few wise decisions. I look at risk as it relates to both commodities and investing in general in Chapter 2.

Looking Ahead: Creating a Financial Road Map

Building wealth through investing takes a lot of time, effort, and discipline — unlike winning the lottery or getting a large inheritance. Achieving your financial goals takes a conscious and systematic effort. Of course, the first part is identifying and establishing your financial goals. These goals may be as diverse as amassing enough money to retire by age 50 and travel the world, to gathering enough money to pay for college, or to making enough money to pass on to your children or grandchildren. Before you start investing in commodities (or any other asset), sit down and figure out clear financial goals. Every individual has different needs and interests. In the following sections, I outline some key points to help you establish your financial goals.

After you identify your goals, you can begin figuring out how to use commodities to achieve those goals. I show you how in the section "Making Room in Your Portfolio for Commodities."

Figuring out your net worth

You need to know where you are before you can determine where you want to go. From a personal finance perspective, you need to know how much you're worth so that you can determine how much capital to allocate to investments, living expenses, retirement, and so on.

You calculate your net worth by subtracting your total liabilities from your total assets. (*Assets* put money in your pocket, whereas *liabilities* remove money from your pocket.)

Fill in the blanks in Table 11-1 to determine the total value of your assets.

Table 11-1	Total Assets
Assets	*Value*
Annuities	$_____
Bonds and other fixed income	$_____
Cash in all checking and savings accounts	$_____
Cash on hand	$_____
Certificates of deposit (CDs)	$_____
Commodity investments	$_____
Futures and options	$_____
Individual retirement accounts (IRAs)	$_____
Life insurance	$_____
Money market funds	$_____
Market value of home	$_____
Market value of other real estate	$_____
Mutual funds	$_____
Pension plans (401(k) and/or 403(b))	$_____
Personal belongings (home furnishings, jewelry, and so on)	$_____

Assets	Value
Stocks and other equity	$_____
Vehicles (car, boat, and so on)	$_____
Other investment assets	$_____
TOTAL VALUE OF ASSETS	$_____

Assets are only one part of the net worth equation. After you calculate your total assets, you need to determine how many liabilities you have. Use Table 11-2 to help you determine your total liabilities.

Table 11-2	Total Liabilities
Liabilities	**Value**
Car loans	$_____
College loans	$_____
Credit card loans	$_____
Mortgage(s)	$_____
Mortgage equity line	$_____
Other loans	$_____
TOTAL VALUE OF LIABILITIES	$_____

After you determine both your total assets and total liabilities, use the following formula to determine your total net worth:

Total net worth = Total assets − Total liabilities

Determining your net worth on a regular basis is important because it allows you to keep track of the balance between your assets and liabilities. Knowing your net worth allows you to then determine which investment strategy to pursue.

The key to increasing your net worth is to increase your assets while reducing your liabilities. Investing helps you increase your assets. Cutting down on living expenses may help you reduce your liabilities.

Identifying your tax bracket

Taxes have a direct impact on how much of your assets you get to keep at the end of the day. You must understand the implications that taxes can have on your portfolio.

How much you pay in taxes is based on your tax bracket. Table 11-3 lists the individual income tax brackets to help you determine how much you'll end up paying in taxes based on your income.

Table 11-3	Federal Income Tax Rate Schedule
Annual Taxable Income	*Tax Level*
$0–$8,375	10%
$8,375–$34,000	15%
$34,000–$82,400	25%
$82,400–$171,850	28%
$171,850–$373,650	33%
$373,650+	35%

The tax rate schedule in Table 11-3, known as Schedule X, applies to you if you're filing as a single person. The Internal Revenue Service (IRS) has a number of different schedules, depending on how you're filing your returns.

✔ **Schedule Y-1:** Married and filing jointly *or* qualifying widow(er)

✔ **Schedule Y-2:** Married and filing separately

✔ **Schedule Z:** Head of household

Tax rates change depending on which schedule you file under. Visit the IRS Web site, at www.irs.gov, or talk to your accountant to find out the tax rates under the different schedules. Because tax rates may change on an annual basis, inquire about these tax issues regularly.

Where you live can also have a big impact on how taxes affect your investments. The following states have no income tax, which means you get to keep more of what you earn!

- ✔ Alaska
- ✔ Florida
- ✔ Nevada
- ✔ New Hampshire
- ✔ South Dakota
- ✔ Tennessee
- ✔ Texas
- ✔ Washington
- ✔ Wyoming

Out of the nine states that don't have personal income taxes, Florida does place a tax on intangible personal property. Thus, items such as stocks, bonds, and mutual funds are subject to taxes. Also note that New Hampshire and Tennessee both tax income earned on interest and dividends.

Investing in commodities, as in any other asset class, has tax implications. I'm not an accountant, and the aim of this book isn't to offer you tax advice, so I recommend that you talk to your accountant before you invest in commodities. Knowing the tax implications before you invest may save you a lot of heartache down the road.

Determining your appetite for risk

Risk is perhaps the single greatest enemy you face as an investor. How wonderful would life be if you could have guaranteed returns without risk? Because that's not possible (and has never been possible), you have to find how to manage, tame, and minimize risk. I devote a whole chapter to managing risk related to commodities (see Chapter 2), but I briefly discuss general portfolio risk in this section.

Your risk tolerance depends on a number of factors that are unique to you as an individual. The first step in determining your risk tolerance is deciding how much risk you're willing to take on. Although no equation or formula can determine risk (it would be nice if there were one), you can use a general rule to identify the percentage of your assets to dedicate to aggressive investments with an elevated risk/reward ratio.

As a general rule, the younger you are, the higher your percentage of assets should be devoted to higher-risk investments. This approach makes sense because if you lose a lot of value, you still have a lot of time ahead of you to recoup your losses. When you're older, however, you don't have as much time to get back your investments.

Table 11-4 gives you a simple guideline to help you determine the percentage of assets that should go into investments with higher returns (and risks), such as stocks, commodities, and real estate. This is *not* a percentage of how much of your portfolio you should invest in commodities; I discuss that percentage in the following section.

Table 11-4 Recommended Percentage of Assets in Growth Investments by Age Group

Age Group	Percentage in Growth Investments
0–20	Up to 90%
20–30	80%–90%
31–40	70%–80%
41–50	60%–70%
51–64	45%–60%
65 and over	Less than 45%

The rules in Table 11-4 aren't set in stone, but you can use them to approximate how much of your assets to place in investments that have a high risk/reward ratio. If your investments are increasing just fine with the percentages you're working with, don't change them! As the saying goes, if it's not broken, don't try to fix it.

Making Room in Your Portfolio for Commodities

One of the most common questions I get from investors is, "How much of my portfolio should I have in commodities?" My answer is usually simple: It depends. To answer that question, you have to take into account a number of factors to determine how much capital to dedicate to commodities.

Personally, my portfolio may include at any one point anywhere between 35 and 50 percent commodities. However, sometimes it's much lower than that — and sometimes almost 90 percent of my portfolio is in commodities!

If you're new to commodities, I recommend starting out with a relatively modest amount — anywhere between 3 and 5 percent of your portfolio — to see how comfortable you feel with this new member of your financial family. Test how commodities contribute to your overall portfolio's performance during one or two investing quarters. If you're satisfied, I recommend that you gradually increase your percentage.

Many investors who like the way commodities anchor their portfolios settle at about 15 percent exposure to commodities. I find that's a pretty good place to be if you're still getting used to commodities. When you see the benefits and realize how much value commodities can provide, I'll bet that number will steadily increase.

Figure 11-1 shows a hypothetical portfolio that includes commodities along with other asset classes. This could be a sample portfolio for an average investor who wants exposure to both liquid and nonliquid (real estate) assets. A diversified portfolio such as this one helps reduce the overall volatility of your market exposures. Having unrelated assets increases your chances of maintaining good returns when a certain asset underperforms.

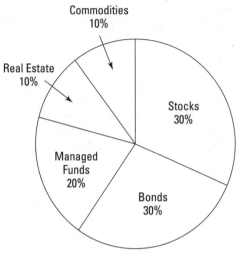

Figure 11-1: Hypothetical portfolio that includes stocks, bonds, commodities, managed funds, and real estate investment allocations.

Fully Exposed: The Top Ways to Get Exposure to Commodities

You have several methods at your disposal, both direct and indirect, for getting exposure to commodities. In this section, I go through the different ways you can invest in commodities.

Looking toward the future with commodity futures

The futures markets are the most direct way to get exposure to commodities. Futures contracts allow you to purchase an underlying commodity for an agreed-upon price in the future. This section lists some ways you can play the futures markets.

Commodity index

Commodity indexes track a basket of commodity futures contracts. Each index uses a different methodology and performs differently than its peers. Commodity indexes are known as passive, long-only investments because they're not

actively managed and they can only buy the underlying commodity; they can't short it.

You can choose from these five major commodity indexes:

- ✔ Deutsche Bank Liquid Commodity Index (DBLCI)
- ✔ Dow Jones–AIG Commodity Index (DJ-AIGCI)
- ✔ Goldman Sachs Commodity Index (GSCI)
- ✔ Reuters/Jefferies Commodity Research Bureau Index (R/J-CRBI)
- ✔ Rogers International Commodity Index (RICI)

Futures commission merchant

Don't be intimidated by the name — a *futures commission
merchant* (FCM) is much like a regular stockbroker. However,
instead of selling stocks, an FCM is licensed to sell futures
contracts, options, and other derivatives to the public.

If you're comfortable trading futures and options contracts,
opening an account with an FCM gives you the most direct
access to the commodity futures markets.

Commodity trading advisor

A *commodity trading advisor* (CTA) is an individual who
manages accounts for clients who trade futures contracts.
The CTA may provide advice on how to place your trades, but
he may also manage your account on your behalf. Be sure to
research the CTA's track record and investment philosophy
so that you know whether it squares with yours.

CTAs may manage accounts for more than one client. However,
they're not allowed to "pool" accounts and share all profits and
losses among clients equally. (This is one of the main differences between a CTA and a CPO, discussed in the next section.)

Chapter 12 can help you identify key elements to look for
when shopping for a CTA.

Commodity pool operator

The *commodity pool operator* (CPO) acts a lot like a CTA,
except that, instead of managing separate accounts, the CPO
has the authority to "pool" all client funds in one account and
trade them as if she were trading one account.

Investing through a CPO offers two advantages over investing through a CTA:

- ✔ Because CPOs can pool funds, they have access to more funds to invest. This pooling provides both leverage and diversification opportunities that smaller accounts don't offer. You can buy a lot more assets with $100,000 than with $10,000.

- ✔ Most CPOs are structured as partnerships, which means that the only money you can lose is your principal. In the world of futures, this is pretty good because, due to margin and the use of leverage, you can end up owing a lot more than the principal if a trade goes sour.

I walk through the pros and cons of investing through a CPO in Chapter 14.

Funding your account with commodity funds

If you think delving into commodity derivatives isn't for you, you can access the commodity markets through funds. If you've invested before, you may be familiar with these two investment vehicles.

Commodity mutual funds

Commodity mutual funds are exactly like average, run-of-the-mill mutual funds, except that they focus specifically on investing in commodities. You can choose from several funds, although the two biggest ones are the PIMCO and the Oppenheimer funds.

A 2005 ruling by the Securities and Exchange Commission (SEC) changed the way mutual funds account for qualifying income. This ruling has put some pressure on funds, particularly PIMCO, to come up with different accounting methods. Find out how such rulings affect your investments.

Exchange-traded funds

Exchange-traded funds (ETFs) have become popular with investors because they provide the benefits of investing in a fund with the ease of trading a stock. This hybrid instrument is becoming one of the best ways for investors to access the commodities markets.

The world of commodity ETFs is fairly new and is constantly changing. Because this is such a dynamic field, I have a section called ETF Watch on my Web site (www.commodities-investors.com) to help you stay up-to-date on everything that's happening in the world of ETFs.

You currently have at your disposal ETFs that track baskets of commodities through commodity indexes, as well as ETFs that track single commodities such as oil, gold, and silver. I list some popular commodity ETFs in Table 11-5.

Table 11-5	Commodity ETFs
ETF	**Description**
Deutsche Bank Commodity Index Tracking Fund (DBC)	Tracks the performance of the Deutsche Bank Commodity Index
US Oil Fund (USO)	Mirrors the movements of the WTI crude oil on the NYMEX
Street Tracks Gold Shares (GLD)	Tracks the performance of gold bullion
iShares COMEX Gold Trust (IAU)	Tracks the performance of gold futures contracts on the COMEX
iShares Silver Trust (SLV)	Tracks the performance of silver

Make sure you examine all fees associated with the ETF before you invest. Check out Chapter 12 for more information on this investment vehicle.

In good company: Investing in commodity companies

Another route you can take to get exposure to commodities is to buy stocks of commodity companies. These companies are generally involved in the production, transformation, or distribution of various commodities.

This route is perhaps the most indirect way of accessing the commodity markets because, in buying a company's stock, you're getting exposure not only to the performance of the underlying commodity that the company is involved in, but also other factors, such as the company's management skills, creditworthiness, and ability to generate cash flow and minimize expenses.

Publicly traded companies

Publicly traded companies can give you exposure to specific sectors of commodities, such as metals, energy, or agricultural products. Within these three categories, you can choose companies that deal with specific methods or commodities, such as refiners of crude oil into finished products or gold-mining companies. If you're considering an equity stake in a commodity company, you need to determine how the company's stock performs relative to the price of the underlying commodity that company is involved in.

There's a relatively strong correlation between the performance of commodity futures contracts and the performance of companies that use these commodities as inputs. So investing in the stock of commodity companies actually gives you pretty good exposure to the underlying commodities themselves. However, you want to be extra careful and to perform thorough due diligence before you invest in these companies. I show you some keys to look for before you invest in such companies in Chapters 6 and 9.

Master limited partnerships

Master limited partnerships (MLPs) are a hybrid instrument that offers you the convenience of trading a partnership like a stock. You get the best of both worlds: the liquidity that comes from being a publicly traded entity and the tax protection of being a partnership.

A big advantage of MLPs is that, as a unit holder, you are taxed at only the individual level. This structure is different than if you invest in a corporation, because cash back to shareholders (in the form of dividends) is taxed at both the corporate level and the individual level. MLPs don't pay any corporate tax, which is a huge benefit for your bottom line.

For an MLP to qualify for these tax breaks, it must generate 90 percent of its income from qualifying sources that relate to commodities, particularly in the oil and gas industry.

Chapter 12

Investing in ETFs and Commodities Indexes

*D*riven by growing investor demand for commodities, many financial institutions are now offering the commodities *exchange-traded fund* (ETF). This new breed of fund enables you to buy into a fund that offers the diversification inherent in a mutual fund and the added benefit of being able to trade that fund like a regular stock. Thus, you get a powerful combination of diversification and liquidity. ETFs are becoming popular with investors because they provide the benefits of investing in a fund with the ease of trading a stock. This hybrid instrument is becoming one of the best ways for investors to access the commodities markets.

If investing were similar to driving a car, the index would be the speedometer — it tells you how fast the car (or the market) is going. Indexes exist for all sorts of assets: The two most well-known indexes track the top 30 blue-chip companies in the United States (Dow Jones Industrial Average) and the 500 largest companies (S&P 500), but others await investors, too.

If you want to measure the performance of commodities, you also have at your disposal indexes that track baskets of commodities. These commodity indexes can be useful for two reasons. First, you can use them as market indicators, to help you gauge where the commodity markets are trading as a whole. Second, because most indexes are tradable instruments (through exchange-traded funds and other investment vehicles), you can profit by investing directly in the index.

This chapter gives you the goods on ETFs and commodity indexes and shows how to profit using these powerful tools.

Getting to Know ETFs

ETFs offer many advantages to investors because they offer exposure to asset classes and specific investments that would otherwise be difficult for the average investor to access, such as uranium or palladium. In addition, they give you a broad diversification platform because they can track a basket of stocks or commodities. This characteristic is a major reason ETFs have become so popular in the last decade, increasing from several dozen to more than 2,500 ETF products.

Unlike a regular mutual fund, in which the net asset value is generally calculated at the end of the trading day, the ETF enables you to trade throughout the day. Furthermore, you can go both long and short with the ETF, something you can't do with regular mutual funds.

It's critical to perform extensive due diligence on any ETF product you're considering for your portfolio. You need a solid understanding of the underlying assets in the ETF. Often beginning investors simply browse the description without getting a good grip on what they're actually buying. For example, the current uranium ETF URA (NYSE: URA) isn't a product that tracks uranium metal prices; it tracks a basket of uranium-mining equities. Folks who don't get into the fine print may miss basic yet critical pieces of information regarding ETFs specifically and broader investment products in general. Go beyond the headlines and into the fine print!

ETFs aren't free, in the sense that they're actively managed products associated with a financial institution. ETF sponsors generally charge an added layer of fees for the convenience of using their products. Therefore, it's imperative to know the types of fees associated with each ETF you purchase. This information is conveniently located in the fund's prospectus.

Deutsche Bank launched the first commodity index ETF in the United States in February 2006. The *Deutsche Bank Commodity Index Tracking Fund* (AMEX: DBC) is listed on the American Stock and Options Exchange (AMEX) and tracks the Deutsche Bank Liquid Commodity Index (DBLCI). The DBLCI, in turn, tracks a basket of six liquid commodities:

- ✔ Light, sweet crude oil (35 percent)
- ✔ Heating oil (20 percent)
- ✔ Aluminum (12.5 percent)
- ✔ Corn (11.25 percent)
- ✔ Wheat (11.25 percent)
- ✔ Gold (10 percent)

You can see the performance of the DBC in Figure 12-1; clearly, the DBC is a superb indicator of the broader commodity markets. The story of commodities since 2005 is characterized by a massive run-up in prices, driven partly by large consumption demands from emerging markets such as China and by speculative activity. That resulted in a massive bursting of asset bubbles in 2008 during the Global Financial Crisis. Commodities, like almost every other tradable asset class, suffered a shocking downward dislocation when liquidity dried up; the DBC portrays this turn of events.

© *John Wiley & Sons, Inc.*

Figure 12-1: Performance of the Deutsche Bank Commodity Index (DBC), 2006–2010.

The DBC ETF is structured as a commodity pool operator (CPO), and the fund invests directly in commodity futures contracts. (See Chapter 14 for more on commodity pools.) To capture additional yields, the energy contracts are rolled monthly; the rest of the contracts are rolled annually. The fund also invests in fixed-income products, including the three-month Treasury bill, which provides an additional yield for investors. With an expense ratio of 1.5 percent, it's a reasonably priced investment.

Accessing Commodity Markets through ETFs

One of the downsides of investing in ETFs is that they can be fairly volatile because they track derivative instruments that trade in the futures markets. A downside of the DBC specifically (see the preceding section) is that it tracks a basket of only six commodities. However, more commodity ETFs are in the pipeline that will offer greater diversification benefits. In Table 12-1, I list some of the more common ETFs available. As you can see, you can now access a broad variety of commodity markets through ETFs, ranging from livestock and natural gas all the way to uranium and palladium.

Table 12-1	Commodity ETFs	
ETF	*Category*	*Ticker*
Dow Jones–AIG Commodity Index Total Return	Broad index	NYSE: DJP
Deutsche Bank Commodity Index Tracking Fund	Broad index	NYSE: DBC
Goldman Sachs Commodity Index Total Return	Broad index	NYSE: GSG
Dow Jones–AIG Agriculture Total Return ETN	Agriculture index	NYSE: JJA
streetTRACKS Gold Shares ETF	Gold	NYSE: GLD
iShares Gold Trust ETF	Gold	NYSE: IAU
iShares Silver Trust Fund	Silver	NYSE: SLV
Dow Jones–AIG Aluminum ETN	Aluminum	NYSE: JJU
United States Natural Gas Fund	Natural gas	NYSE: UNG
United States Oil Fund	Crude oil	NYSE: USO

ETF	Category	Ticker
Dow Jones–AIG Livestock Total Return ETN	Livestock index	NYSE: COW
ETFS Physical Palladium Shares ETF	Palladium	NYSE: PALL
ETFS Physical Platinum Shares ETF	Platinum	NYSE: PPLT
Global X Global Gold Explorers ETF	Gold exploration	NYSE: GLDX
Global X Global Silver Explorers ETF	Silver exploration	NYSE: SIL
Global X Lithium ETF	Lithium metal	NYSE: LIT
Global X Uranium ETF	Uranium metal	NYSE: URA
Emerging Global Energy Titans Index	Energy companies	NYSE: EEO

As commodities become a more accepted asset class, I expect more ETFs to launch and be available for you to trade. For the latest, check out www.commodities-investors.com.

Taking a Look at Leveraged ETFs

A new breed of ETFs is emerging and is having a major impact on the ETF and commodity landscapes: *leveraged* ETFs. As the name suggests, leveraged ETFs (or LETFs, for short) seek to boost the returns of the underlying asset by using an added layer of leverage. LETFs often do this through futures, options, and swaps, to enhance returns. The leverage can go both ways, both long and short, so it has a certain degree of versatility that investors find appealing and that has boosted the popularity of this new breed.

However, LETFs have also come under strong criticism by industry insiders for the massive use of leverage. Leverage is a double-edged sword, possibly enhancing your returns on the way up, but ushering in potential catastrophe on the way down. Professional investment advisors warn their clients about the responsible use of leverage, and if you're not an experienced trader, tread carefully with LETFs.

If you're gung-ho about using LETFs, consult your financial advisor and carefully read the fine print in the prospectus to get a solid understanding of the type and degree of leverage used. In some cases, ETFs use *double* leverage — that's right, leverage × 2 — to further enhance returns. My advice is, if you don't have a crystal clear grasp of leverage, steer clear of products that use this mechanism.

Checking Out Commodity Indexes

A commodity index tracks the price of a futures contract of an underlying physical commodity on a designated exchange. When you invest through one of the commodity indexes in this chapter, you're actually investing in the futures markets.

Indexes are known as passive, long-only investments, for two reasons: No one is actively trading the index, and the index tracks only the long performance of a commodity. It doesn't track commodities that are *short* (a sophisticated strategy meant to profit when prices go down).

Why indexes are useful

Using commodity indexes is a good way to determine where the commodity markets are heading. Just as stock indexes allow you to identify broad market movements (which then enables you to implement and update your investment strategy accordingly), commodity indexes give you a way to measure the broad movements of the commodities markets.

In essence, a commodity index gives you a snapshot of the current state of the commodities market. You can use an index in one of three ways:

- ✔ **Benchmark:** You can use a commodity index to compare the performance of commodities as an asset class with the performance of other asset classes, such as stocks and bonds.

- ✔ **Indicator:** You can use the commodity index as an indicator of economic activity, possible inflationary pressures, and the state of global economic production.

✔ **Investment vehicle:** Because a commodity index tracks the performance of specific futures contracts, you can replicate the performance of the index by trading the contracts it tracks. You can invest in a commodity index both directly (by buying the contracts) and indirectly (via mutual funds); I discuss those options in depth in the following section.

How to make money by using an index

You can invest through a commodity index by using a number of methods. You can choose from five widely followed commodity indexes (I cover these in the section "Cataloguing Five Major Indexes," later in this chapter), and each one is tracked and traded differently.

Consider a few ways you can invest through a commodity index:

✔ **Own the futures contracts.** One of the most direct ways of tracking the performance of an index is to own the contracts the index tracks. To do this, you must have a *futures account.* (Refer to Chapter 13 to find out how to open a futures account.)

✔ **Invest with a third-party manager.** Many money managers use commodity indexes as the basis of their investment strategy. Some of these vehicles include mutual funds, commodity pools, and commodity trading advisors. (For more on selecting the right manager, be sure to read Chapter 14.)

✔ **Own futures contracts of the index.** A few commodity indexes have futures contracts that track their performance. When you buy the futures contract of the index, it's similar to buying all the commodity futures contracts the index trades!

✔ **Make use of exchange-traded funds.** ETFs, as they're known on Wall Street, are a fairly new breed of investment that tracks the performance of a fund through the convenience of trading a stock. ETFs are a popular alternative for folks who don't want to trade futures.

Here I list only a few ways you can get exposure to commodity indexes. As commodities become more popular with the investing community, expect to see more ways to get access to indexes. To keep track of all the new developments in index investing, keep checking my Web site, at www.commodities-investors.com.

Uncovering the Anatomy of a Commodity Index

As an investor interested in making money through index investing, you have five commodity indexes at your disposal. Although the composition and structure of every index is different, the aim is the same: to track a basket of commodities. Before you get into specific commodity indexes, watch out for these pitfalls when shopping for an index:

- ✓ **Components:** Each index follows a specific methodology to determine which commodities are part of the index. Some indexes, such as the S&P GSCI (see the following section), include commodities based on their global *production value*. Other indexes, such as the DBLCI, include commodities based on their *liquidity* and *representational value* of a component class, such as picking gold to represent metals and choosing oil as a representative of the energy market.

- ✓ **Weightings:** Some indexes follow a *production-weighted methodology,* in which weights are assigned to each commodity based on its proportional production in the world. Other indexes choose *component weightings* based on the liquidity of the commodity's futures contract. In addition, some weightings are fixed over a predetermined period of time, whereas others fluctuate to reflect changes in actual production values.

- ✓ **Rolling methodology:** Because the index's purpose is to track the performance of commodities and not take actual delivery of the commodity, the futures contracts that the index tracks must be rolled over from the *current-month* contract to the *front-month* contract (the upcoming trading month). Because this rolling process provides a *roll yield* (a yield that results from the price differential between the current and front months), you need to examine each index's policy on rolling. You can find this information in the index brochure.

✔ **Rebalancing features:** Every index reviews its components and their weightings on a regular basis to maintain an index that reflects actual values in the global commodities markets. Some indexes rebalance annually; other indexes rebalance more frequently. Before you invest in an index, find out when it's rebalanced and what methodology it uses to rebalance.

Although each index is constructed differently, all indexes have to follow certain criteria to determine whether a commodity will be included in the index:

✔ **Tradability:** The commodities have to be traded on a designated exchange and must have a futures contract assigned to them.

✔ **Deliverability:** The contracts that go into the index must be for an underlying commodity that has the potential to be delivered. This eliminates the inclusion of futures contracts that represent financial instruments, such as economic indicators, interest rates, and other "financials."

✔ **Liquidity:** The market for the underlying commodity has to be liquid enough to allow investors to move in and out of their positions without facing liquidity crunches, such as not being able to find a buyer or seller.

Cataloguing Five Major Indexes

In the following sections, I go through each of the five major commodity indexes you can invest in. Each one is unique, so you can be sure to find one that best suits your needs.

The S&P Goldman Sachs Commodity Index

The S&P *Goldman Sachs Commodity Index* (S&P GSCI) is one of the most closely watched indexes in the market. Launched in 1992 by the investment bank Goldman Sachs, it tracks the performance of 24 commodity futures contracts. In 2007,

Standard & Poor's (S&P) purchased the original GSCI from Goldman Sachs and is now responsible for its operations. The S&P GSCI is the most heavily tracked index. As of 2006, investors had poured in $50 billion to track it; by 2010, that figure was $65 billion.

The S&P GSCI is a production-weighted index because it assigns different weights to different commodities proportional to their current global production quantity, a method known as *global production weighting*. As such, the index assigns more weight to crude oil than cocoa, to reflect actual world production figures — there's a lot more crude oil produced in the world than cocoa.

To calculate the contract production weight of each commodity (the percentage of a commodity assigned to the index), the S&P GSCI takes the average of that commodity's global production over the previous five years. The main advantage of using a five-year average over a one-year average is that it takes into account any statistical aberrations related to the production of the specific commodity. For example, if a natural disaster affected the production of a particular commodity during one year, the five-year average would reflect that change but still maintain a heavy weighting on that commodity because that event was an aberration.

Table 12-2 lists the actual commodity futures contracts that make up the S&P GSCI, along with their correspondent weighting in the index. I also list the exchange on which they trade, in case you want to purchase these contracts.

Table 12-2			S&P GSCI Components		
Commodity	*Exchange*	*Weight*	*Commodity*	*Exchange*	*Weight*
Chicago wheat	CME	2.47%	Gas–oil	ICE	4.41%
Kansas wheat	KBOT	0.90%	Unleaded gas	CME	7.84%
Corn	CME	2.46%	WTI crude oil	CME	30.05%
Soybeans	CME	1.77%	Brent crude oil	ICE	13.81%
Coffee	CSC	0.80%	Natural gas	CME	10.30%
Sugar	CSC	1.30%	Aluminum	LME	2.88%

Commodity	Exchange	Weight	Commodity	Exchange	Weight
Cocoa	CSC	0.23%	Copper	LME	2.37%
Cotton	NYC	0.99%	Lead	LME	0.29%
Lean hogs	CME	2.00%	Nickel	LME	0.82%
Live cattle	CME	2.88%	Zinc	LME	0.54%
Feeder cattle	CME	0.78%	Gold	CME	1.73%
Heating oil	CME	8.16%	Silver	CME	0.20%

Because futures contracts have an expiration date, they must be rolled on a regular basis. Contracts such as the crude oil futures are rolled monthly because they expire every month. However, some contracts have contract expiration dates only during certain months of the year. These contracts, such as the contracts for cotton or gold, are rolled according to the available monthly contract trade.

The S&P GSCI has a futures contract that tracks the index's performance. You can buy this contract on the Chicago Mercantile Exchange (CME). If you have a futures trading account (you find out how to open one in Chapter 13), you can simply buy this contract to get direct access to the S&P GSCI. The ticker symbol for the S&P GSCI on the CME is GI.

Another way to access the S&P GSCI is to invest in a managed fund that tracks its performance. One such fund is the Oppenheimer Real Asset Fund (discussed in Chapter 13). The Oppenheimer Fund mirrors the performance of the S&P GSCI. But as a general rule, managed funds don't identically replicate the performance of an index because of external factors such as loads, management fees, and other expenses related to the management of the fund.

Reuters/Jefferies Commodity Research Bureau Index

Created in 1957 as the Commodity Research Bureau's official commodity-tracking index, this index is the oldest commodity index in the world. The original index received a makeover in 2005 when it was renamed the *Reuters/Jefferies Commodity Research Bureau Index* (CRB) — quite a mouthful!

The CRB index is widely followed by institutional investors and economists; of all the indexes, it's perhaps the most widely used as an economic benchmark, although the S&P GSCI and the DJ/AIGCI (introduced in the next section) are also widely used references.

The CRB index currently tracks a basket of 19 commodities, which are selected based on their liquidity and production value. This index is unique because it is the only index that uses a *tiered methodology* of distributing weights to commodities. This hybrid approach gives a production value weight to energy products, while assigning fixed weights to other commodities. The components and their weightings are reviewed annually. Table 12-3 lists the index tiers and the commodities the index tracks.

Table 12-3   CRB Index Tiers and Components

Tiers	Commodity	Weight	Exchange
Tier I	WTI crude oil	23%	CME
	Heating oil	5%	CME
	Unleaded gas	5%	CME
Tier II	Natural gas	6%	CME
	Corn	6%	CME
	Soybeans	6%	CME
	Live cattle	6%	CME
	Gold	6%	CME
	Aluminum	6%	LME
	Copper	6%	CME
Tier III	Sugar	5%	ICE
	Cotton	5%	ICE
	Cocoa	5%	ICE
	Coffee	5%	ICE
Tier IV	Nickel	1%	LME
	Wheat	1%	CME
	Lean hogs	1%	CME
	Orange juice	1%	ICE
	Silver	1%	CME

Dow Jones–AIG Commodity Index

With approximately $31 billion tracking it (2010 figures), the *Dow Jones–AIG Commodity Index* (DJ-AIGCI) is one of the most widely followed indexes in the market. The DJ-AIGCI places a premium on liquidity but also chooses commodities based on their production value.

The DJ-AIGCI is one of the few indexes that places a *floor* and *ceiling* on individual commodities and component classes. For example, no component class (such as energy or metals) is allowed to account for more than 33 percent of the index weighting. Another rule is that no single commodity may make up less than 2 percent of the index's total weighting. The DJ-AIGCI follows these rules to ensure that all commodities are well represented and that no commodity or component class dominates the index.

The component weightings are rebalanced annually. Currently, the index tracks a group of 19 publicly traded commodities, listed in Table 12-4.

Table 12-4		DJ-AIGCI Components	
Commodity	*Weight*	*Commodity*	*Weight*
Natural gas	12.32%	Aluminum	6.90%
WTI crude oil	12.78%	Copper	5.88%
Unleaded gas	4.05%	Zinc	2.70%
Heating oil	3.84%	Nickel	2.66%
Live cattle	6.09%	Gold	6.22%
Lean hogs	4.35%	Silver	2.00%
Wheat	4.77%	Sugar	2.96%
Corn	5.87%	Cotton	3.16%
Soybeans	7.76%	Coffee	2.93%
Soybean oil	2.76%		

One way to access the commodities listed in the DJ-AIGCI is to invest in a mutual fund that tracks it. One of the largest commodity mutual funds, the *PIMCO Commodity Real Return Fund,* uses the DJ-AIGCI as its benchmark. Therefore, you get a very high correlation between the performance of the index and the performance of the fund. Turn to Chapter 11 to find out more about the PIMCO fund.

Another way to access the DJ-AIGCI is through the CME, which offers a futures contract that tracks the performance of the DJ-AIGCI. It's similar to the S&P GSCI contract on the CME. The ticker symbol for the DJ-AIGCI on the CME is AI.

Rogers International Commodities Index

With a grand total of 35 listed commodities, the *Rogers International Commodities Index* (RICI) tracks the most commodities among the different indexes. The RICI is the brainchild of famed commodities investor Jim Rogers, who launched the index to achieve the widest exposure to commodities.

As with the other commodity indexes, the RICI includes traditional commodities such as crude oil, natural gas, and silver. However, it also includes quite exotic commodities, including silk and adzuki beans. If you're looking for the broadest exposure to commodities, the RICI is probably your best bet.

The RICI was launched in 1998 and has performed extremely well. The RICI is a production-weighted index, assigning weightings to component classes based on their actual global production value and rebalancing the index every December. Table 12-5 lists the RICI components and their index weighting.

If you want to invest in the RICI, you can do so through the *RICI TRAKRS* offered by the CME. *TRAKRS* (pronounced "trackers") are similar to the futures contracts offered by the CME. To trade the RICI TRAKRS on the CME, use the ticker symbol RCI.

Deutsche Bank Liquid Commodity Index

Launched in 2003 by Deutsche Bank, the *Deutsche Bank Liquid Commodity Index* (DBLCI) is the new kid on the index block

Table 12-5		RICI Components	
Commodity	*Weight*	*Commodity*	*Weight*
Crude oil	35%	Sugar	2%
Wheat	7%	Platinum	1.80%
Corn	4.75%	Live hogs	1%
Aluminum	4%	Cocoa	1%
Copper	4%	Nickel	1%
Cotton	4%	Tin	1%
Heating oil	3.75%	Rubber	1%
Unleaded gas	3.75%	Lumber	1%
Natural gas	3%	Soybean meal	0.75%
Soybeans	3%	Canola	0.67%
Gold	3%	Orange juice	0.66%
Live cattle	2%	Rice	0.50%
Coffee	2%	Adzuki beans	0.50%
Zinc	2%	Oats	0.50%
Silver	2%	Palladium	0.30%
Lead	2%	Barley	0.27%
Soybean oil	2%	Silk	0.05%

and has the most distinct approach to tracking commodity
futures contracts. The DBLCI tracks just six commodity
contracts: two in energy, two in metals, and two in agricultural products.

The weighting of the DBLCI is done at the end of the year, and
it seeks to reflect global production values. Hence, as with the
other production-weighted indexes (such as the S&P GSCI),
it's also overweight energy because this reflects the current
production values in the world.

Table 12-6 lists the commodities that make up the component
classes of the DBLCI.

Table 12-6	DBLCI Components	
Commodity	*Exchange*	*Weight*
WTI crude oil	CME	35%
Heating oil	CME	20%
Aluminum	LME	12.5%
Corn	CME	11.25%
Wheat	CME	11.25%
Gold	CME	10%

With so few underlying commodities, you may be asking whether the DBLCI offers a broad and diverse enough exposure to the commodities markets. One of the advantages of the DBLCI is that it chooses only the most *liquid* and *representative* commodities in their respective component classes.

For example, the WTI Crude Oil contract is indicative of where the energy complex is moving. So instead of including unleaded gas, propane, natural gas, and other energy contracts, the DBLCI relies on WTI as a benchmark to achieve representation in the energy market as a whole. This approach is unique in the world of commodity indexes: The index can track the commodities markets by monitoring the performance of only a small number of commodities. This "less is more" approach is also helpful for individual investors who prefer to track indexes by buying the index contracts: Instead of buying 19 contracts, you have to buy only 6 contracts to mirror the index's performance.

The energy contracts of the DBLCI are rolled monthly; the metal and agricultural contracts are rolled annually.

The DBLCI is the first commodity index to have its performance tracked by an exchange-traded fund (ETF). You can buy the ETF and get exposure to the DBLCI on the American Stock and Options Exchange (AMEX). Deutsche Bank also manages this fund, whose ticker symbol is DBC.

Determining Which Index to Use

With so many indexes to choose from, how do you decide which one to follow? Generally, the S&P Goldman Sachs Commodity Index (S&P GSCI) is the most tracked index in the market — it has the most funds following, or tracking, its performance. As of 2010, more than $85 billion in assets tracked its performance, and this number is still growing monthly. The index is pretty popular with institutional and, increasingly, individual investors. It's also perhaps the easiest one to follow because you can track it by investing through the Oppenheimer Real Asset Fund, as well as through the S&P GSCI futures contracts on the CME.

Although the S&P GSCI is the most widely tracked index, the most closely *watched* index (there's a difference) is the Reuters/Jefferies CRB Index. The CRB Index is a global benchmark for what the commodities markets are doing. As such, it is the equivalent of the Dow Jones Industrial Average in the commodity world: When investors want to gauge where the commodity markets are heading, they usually turn to the CRB Index. In addition, when analysts or journalists discuss the performance of the commodities markets, they usually refer to the CRB Index.

Investors who don't trade futures or don't feel comfortable investing in an index through a mutual fund can always choose to invest in an index through ETFs, which offer the convenience of trading complex financial instruments with the ease of trading stocks. Currently, the DBLCI is the only index tracked by an ETF, the DBC. Buying the DBC is as simple as logging into your brokerage account or calling your broker and placing an order for the number of DBC units you want to purchase. An ETF is in the works to track the S&P GSCI, and I expect to see more ETFs that track these commodity indexes as more investors seek access to this area of the market.

Chapter 13

Getting a Grip on Futures and Options

. . . .

In This Chapter

▶ Figuring out futures contracts

▶ Trading on margin

▶ Identifying market movements

▶ Deciphering options contracts

. . . .

Some investors think that "futures and options" and "commodities" are basically the same, but they're not. *Commodities* are a class of assets that includes energy, metals, agricultural products, and similar items. *Futures* and *options* are investment vehicles through which you can invest in commodities. Think of it this way: If commodities were a place, futures and options would be the vehicle you'd use to get there. In addition to commodities, futures and options allow you to invest in a variety of other asset classes, such as stocks, indexes, currencies, bonds, and even interest rates, often referred to as financial futures.

 In Wall Street lingo, futures and options are known as *derivatives* because they *derive* their value from an underlying financial instrument such as a stock, bond, or commodity. However, futures and options are different financial instruments with singular structures and uses — but I'm getting ahead of myself.

My aim in this chapter isn't to make you an expert in trading these sophisticated financial instruments, but to introduce you to these vehicles so that you have a working knowledge of what they are. If you then choose to use them in your trading strategy, you'll at least have a good understanding of how to best utilize them. Or if you decide to hire a professional money manager to invest in the futures markets for you, you'll know the lingo and key concepts so you can ask the right questions. I include a comprehensive list of money managers who specialize in helping investors invest in the futures markets on my Web site, www.commodities-investors.com. I also discuss how to go about choosing a money manager in Chapter 14.

The Future Looks Bright: How to Trade Futures Contracts

The futures market is divided into two segments: one that's regulated and another one that's unregulated. Trading in the regulated portion of the futures market is done through designated commodity futures exchanges such as the New York Board of Trade (NYBOT) — now part of the Intercontinental Exchange (ICE) — and the Chicago Mercantile Exchange (CME). Trading in the unregulated portion of the futures market is done by individual parties outside the purview of the exchanges. This is known as the *over-the-counter (OTC) market.*

The futures market is the opposite of the cash market, often known as the *spot market,* because transactions take place right away, or on the spot.

A *futures contract* is a highly standardized financial instrument in which two parties enter into an agreement to exchange an underlying security (such as soybeans, palladium, or ethanol) at a mutually agreed-upon price at a specific time in the future — which is why it's called a futures contract.

Futures contracts, by definition, trade on designated commodity futures exchanges, such as the London Metal Exchange (LME) or the Chicago Mercantile Exchange (CME). The exchanges provide liquidity and transparency to all market participants. However, the structure of the futures market is such that only about 20 percent of market activity takes place in the exchange arena. The overwhelming majority of transactions in the futures markets take place in the OTC market. The OTC market isn't regulated or monitored by the exchanges, and it usually involves two market participants that establish the terms of their agreements through forward contracts. *Forwards* are similar to futures contracts, except that they trade in the OTC market and thus allow the parties to come up with flexible and individualized terms for their agreements. Generally, the OTC market isn't suitable for individual investors who seek speculative opportunities because it consists primarily of large commercial users (such as oil companies and airlines) who use it solely for hedging purposes.

In this chapter, I focus on derivatives that trade on the commodity exchanges. I don't focus on the OTC market because it doesn't lend itself to trading by individual investors. So when I refer to the "futures market" in this chapter, I'm talking about the trading activity in the designated commodity futures exchanges.

Despite the fact that futures contracts are designed to accommodate delivery of physical commodities, such delivery rarely takes place because the primary purpose of the futures markets is to minimize risk and maximize profits. The futures market, unlike the cash or spot market, isn't intended to serve as the primary exchange of physical commodities. Instead, it's a market where buyers and sellers transact with each other for hedging and speculative purposes. Out of the billions of contracts traded on commodity futures exchanges each year, only about 2 percent of these contracts result in the actual physical delivery of a commodity.

In the land of futures contracts, both the buyer and the seller have the right *and* the obligation to fulfill the contract's terms. This process works differently than in the realm of options: With options, the buyer has the right but *not* the obligation to exercise the option, and the seller has the obligation but *not* the right to fulfill her contractual obligations. This scenario can get a little confusing, I know! I dig deeper into these issues in the section "Trading with Options."

The competition: Who trades futures?

Essentially, two types of folks trade futures contracts. The first are commercial producers and consumers of commodities who use the futures markets to stabilize either their costs (in the case of consumers) or their revenues (in the case of producers). The second group consists of individual traders, investment banks, and other financial institutions who are interested in using the futures markets as a way of generating trading profits. Both groups take advantage of the futures markets' liquidity and leverage (which I discuss in the following sections) to implement their trading strategies.

If you ever get involved in the futures markets, it's important to know who you're up against. I examine the role of these hedgers and speculators in the following sections so you're ready to deal with the competition.

Getting over the hedge

Hedgers are the actual producers and consumers of commodities. Both producers and consumers enter the futures markets with the aim of reducing price volatility in the commodities they buy or sell. Hedging gives these commercial enterprises the opportunity to reduce the risk associated with daily price fluctuations by establishing fixed prices of primary commodities for months, sometimes even years, in advance.

Hedgers can be on either side of a transaction in the futures market, the *buy side* or the *sell side.* Consider a few examples of entities that use the futures markets for hedging purposes:

- Farmers who want to establish steady prices for their products use futures contracts to sell their products to consumers at a fixed price for a fixed period of time, thus guaranteeing a fixed stream of revenues.

- Electric utility companies that supply power to residential customers can buy electricity on the futures markets, to keep their costs fixed and protect their bottom line.

- Transportation companies whose business depends on the price of fuel get involved in the futures markets to maintain fixed costs of fuel over specific periods of time.

The truth about speculators

For some reason, the term *speculator* carries some negative connotation, as if speculating is a sinful or immoral act. In reality, speculators play an important and necessary role in the global financial system. In fact, whenever you buy a stock or a bond, you're speculating. When you think prices are going up, you buy. When they're going down, you sell. The process of figuring out where prices are heading and how to profit from this is the essence of speculation. So we're all speculators!

In the futures markets, speculators provide much-needed liquidity that allows the many market players to match their buy and sell orders. Speculators, often simply known as *traders,* buy and sell futures contracts, options, and other exchange-traded products through an electronic platform or a broker, to profit from price fluctuations. A trader who thinks that the price of crude oil is going up will buy a crude oil futures contract to try to profit from his hunch. This action adds liquidity to the markets, which is valuable because liquidity is a prerequisite for the smooth and efficient functioning of the futures markets.

When markets are liquid, you know that you'll be able to find a buyer or a seller for your contracts. You also know that you'll get a reasonable price because liquidity offers you a large pool of market participants competing for your contracts. Finally, liquidity means that when a number of participants are transacting in the marketplace, prices aren't going to be subject to extremely wild and unpredictable price fluctuations. This doesn't mean that liquidity eliminates volatility, but it certainly helps reduce it.

At the end of the day, having a large number of market participants is positive, and speculators play an important role with the liquidity they add to the futures markets.

Contract specs: Keeping track of all the moving pieces

Trading futures contracts takes a lot of discipline, patience, and coordination. One of the biggest deterrents to participating in the futures markets is the number of moving pieces you have to constantly monitor. In this section, I go through the many pieces you have to keep track of if you decide to trade futures.

Because futures contracts can be traded on only designated and regulated exchanges, these contracts are highly standardized. *Standardization* simply means that these contracts are based on a uniform set of rules. For example, the CME crude oil contract is standardized because it represents a specific grade of crude (West Texas Intermediate) and a specific size (1,000 barrels). Therefore, you can expect all CME crude contracts to represent 1,000 barrels of West Texas Intermediate crude oil. In other words, the contract you purchase won't be for 1,000 barrels of Nigerian Bonny Light, another grade of crude oil.

The regulatory bodies that are responsible for overseeing and monitoring trading activities on commodity futures exchanges are the Commodity Futures Trading Commission (CFTC) and the National Futures Association (NFA).

The buyer of a futures contract is known as the *holder;* when you buy a futures contract, you're essentially "going long" the commodity. The seller of a futures contract is referred to as the *underwriter* or *writer.* If you sell a futures contract, you're holding a short position. Remember that "going long" simply means you're on the buy side of a transaction; conversely, "going short" means you're on the sell side. In other words, when you "go long," you expect prices to rise, and when you "go short," you expect prices to decrease.

Underlying asset

The *underlying asset* is the financial instrument that the futures contract represents. The underlying asset can be anything from crude oil to platinum, to soybeans, to propane. Because futures contracts are traded on designated exchanges, every exchange offers different types of assets you can trade. For a list of these assets, be sure to read Chapter 12.

Futures contracts can be used to trade all sorts of assets, not just traditional commodities like oil and gold. Futures can be used to trade interest rates, indexes, currencies, equities, and a host of other assets. Some futures contracts even allow you to trade weather!

Before you place your order, make sure that you're very clear about the underlying commodity you want to trade. Specify on which exchange you want your order executed. This is important because you have contracts for the same commodities that trade on different exchanges. For example, aluminum futures contracts are traded on both the CME and the LME.

When you're placing an order for an aluminum contract, it's important to specify where you want to buy the contract: either on the COMEX or on the LME.

Underlying quantity

The contract size, also known as the *trading unit,* is how much of the underlying asset the contract represents. To meet certain standards, all futures contracts have a predetermined and fixed size. For example, one futures contract for ethanol traded on the Chicago Board of Trade is the equivalent of one rail car of ethanol, which is approximately 29,000 gallons.

The light, sweet crude oil contract on the CME represents 1,000 U.S. barrels, which is the equivalent of 42,000 gallons. The futures contract for frozen pork bellies represents 40,000 pounds of pork.

Make sure that you know the exact amount of underlying commodity the contract represents before you purchase a futures contract.

Because more individual investors want to trade futures contracts, many exchanges are now offering contracts with smaller sizes, which means that the contracts cost less. The CME, for instance, now offers the miNY Light Sweet Crude Oil contract, which represents 500 barrels of oil and is half the price of its traditional crude oil contract.

Product grade

Imagine that you placed an order for a Ford Mustang and instead got a Ford Taurus. You'd be pretty upset, right? To avoid unpleasant surprises if delivery of a physical commodity actually takes place, exchanges require that all contracts represent a standard product grade. For instance, gasoline futures traded on the CME are based on contract specifications for New York Harbor Unleaded Gasoline. This grade is a uniform grade of gasoline widely used across the East Coast, which is transported to New York Harbor from refineries in the East Coast and the Gulf of Mexico. Thus, if delivery of a CME gasoline futures contract takes place, you can expect to receive New York Harbor Unleaded Gas.

If your sole purpose is to speculate and you're not intending to have gasoline or soybeans delivered, knowing the product grade isn't as important as if you were taking physical delivery of the commodity. However, it's always good to know what kind of product you're actually trading.

Price quote

Most futures contracts are priced in U.S. dollars, but some contracts are priced in other currencies, such as the pound sterling or the Japanese yen. The price quote really depends on which exchange you're buying or selling the futures contract from. Keep in mind that if you're trading futures in a foreign currency, you're potentially exposing yourself to currency exchange risks.

Price limits

Price limits help you determine the value of the contract. Every contract has a minimum and maximum price increment, also known as *tick size*. Contracts move in ticks, which is the amount by which the futures contract increases or decreases with every transaction. Most stocks, for example, move in cents. In futures, most contracts move in larger dollar amounts, reflecting the size of the contract. In other words, one tick represents different values for different contracts.

For example, the *minimum tick size* of the ethanol futures contract on the CME is $29 per contract. This means every contract will move in increments of $29. On the other hand, the *maximum tick size* for ethanol on the CME is $4,350, meaning that if the tick size is greater than $4,350, trading will be halted. Exchanges step in when contracts are experiencing extreme volatility, to calm the markets.

The exchanges establish minimum and maximum tick sizes based on the settlement price during the previous day's trading session. Determining the value of the tick allows you to quantify the price swings of the contract on any given trading session.

Trading months

Although you can trade futures contracts practically around the clock, certain commodities are available for delivery only during certain months.

For instance, frozen pork bellies on the CME are listed for the months of February, March, May, July, and August. This means that you can trade a July contract at any given point, but you cannot trade a June contract — a contract that's deliverable in June — because that contract doesn't exist. On the other hand, crude oil on the CME is available all 12 months of the year.

Check the contract listing before you trade so you know for which delivery months you can trade the contracts.

The *front month* is simply the upcoming delivery month. For example, June is the front month during the May trading session.

Delivery location

In case of actual delivery, exchanges designate areas where the physical exchange of commodities actually takes place. For instance, delivery of the CME's WTI crude oil contract takes place in Cushing, Oklahoma, which is a major transportation hub for crude oil in the United States.

Last trading day

All futures contracts must expire at some point. The *last trading day* is the absolute latest time you have to trade that particular contract. Trading days change from exchange to exchange and from contract to contract. Be sure to check out the contract specifications at the different exchanges for information on the last trading day.

Trading hours

Before the days of electronic trading, contracts were traded through the open outcry system during specific time periods. Now, with the advent of electronic trading, you have more time to trade the contracts. Check the exchange Web sites for information on trading hours.

Knowing at what times to place your trades has a direct impact on your bottom line because the number of market participants varies throughout the day. Ideally, you'd like to execute your orders when there are the most buyers and sellers because this increases your chances of getting the best price for your contracts.

For a Few Dollars Less: Trading Futures on Margin

One of the unique characteristics of futures contracts is the ability to trade with margin. If you've ever traded stocks, you know that *margin* is the amount of borrowed money you use to pay for stock. Margin in the futures markets is slightly different than stock market margin.

In the futures markets, *margin* refers to the minimum amount of capital that must be available in your account for you to trade futures contracts. Think of margin as collateral that allows you to participate in the futures markets.

 ✔ **Initial margin:** The minimum amount of capital you need in your account to trade futures contracts

 ✔ **Maintenance margin:** The subsequent amount of capital you must contribute to your account to maintain the minimum margin requirements

Margin requirements are established for every type of contract by the exchange on which those contracts are traded. However, the futures broker you use to place your order may have different margin requirements. Make sure you find out what those requirements are before you start trading.

In the stock market, capital gains and losses are calculated after you close out your position. In the futures market, capital gains and losses are calculated at the end of the trading day and credited to or debited from your account. If you experience a loss in your positions on any given day, you receive a *margin call,* which means that you have to replenish your account to meet the minimum margin requirements if you want to keep trading.

Trading on margin provides you with a lot of leverage because you need to put up only relatively small amounts of capital as collateral to invest in significant dollar amounts of a commodity. For example, if you want to trade the soybean futures contracts on the CME, the initial margin requirement is $1,100. With this small amount, you can control a CME soybeans futures contract that has a value of approximately $28,400 (5,000 bushels at $5.68 per bushel)! This translates to a minimum margin requirement of less than 4 percent!

Margin is a double-edged sword because both profits and losses are amplified to large degrees. If you're on the right side of a trade, you're going to make a lot of money. However, you're also in a position to lose much more than your initial investment if things don't go your way. Knowing how to use margin properly is absolutely critical. I discuss in depth how to use leverage responsibly in Chapter 2.

Figuring Out Where the Futures Market Is Heading

You need to be familiar with a couple of technical terms related to movements in the futures markets if you want to successfully trade futures contracts. (Even by Wall Street standards, these terms are kind of out there.)

Contango: It takes two to tango

Futures markets, by definition, are predicated on the future price of a commodity. Analyzing where the future price of a commodity is heading is what futures trading is all about. Because futures contracts are available for different months throughout the year, the price of the contracts changes from month to month. When the *front month* trades higher than the current month, this market condition is known as *contango*. The market is also in contango when the price of the front month is higher than the spot market, and also when late delivery months are higher than near delivery months.

As the contract extends into the future, the price of the contract increases. Contango is thus a bullish indicator, showing that the market expects the price of the futures contract to increase steadily into the future.

Backwardation: One step forward, two steps back

Backwardation is the opposite of contango. When a market is experiencing backwardation, the contracts for future months are decreasing in value relative to the current and most recent months. The spot price is thus greater than the front month, which is greater than future delivery months. A market in backwardation is a bearish sign because traders expect prices over the long term to decrease.

Trading with Options

There's a big difference between futures and options. Often folks think of futures and options as being one and the same — that's understandable, because whenever you hear "futures," "options" is never too far behind! However, as I explain in the following sections, futures and options are different financial instruments with singular structures and uses. Realizing this difference right off the bat will help you understand these financial instruments better.

Futures give the *holder* (buyer) and *underwriter* (seller) both the right *and* the obligation to fulfill the contract's obligations. Options give the holder the right (or option) but not the obligation to exercise the contract. The underwriter of the option, on the other hand, is required to fulfill the contract's obligations if the holder chooses to exercise the contract.

When you're buying an option, you're essentially paying for the right to buy or sell an underlying security at a specific point in time at an agreed-upon price. The price you pay for the right to exercise that option is known as the *premium.*

The technically correct way of thinking about options is as "options on futures contracts." In other words, the options contracts give you the option to buy futures contracts for commodities such as wheat and zinc. These options are different than stock options, which give you the option to purchase stocks. In this section, I examine options on futures contracts because that's the focus of this chapter. If you want an overview of stock options, I recommend *Stock Options For Dummies,* by Alan R. Simon (Wiley).

Following options in action

Understanding options can be challenging because they're, in fact, derivatives used to trade other derivatives (futures contracts). So here's an example that applies the concept of options to a real-world situation.

You walk into a car dealership and see the car of your dreams: It's shiny and beautiful, and you know you'll look great in it! Unfortunately, it costs $100,000, and you can't spend that amount of money on a car right now. However, you're due for a large bonus at work — or you just made a killing trading commodities, take your pick! — and you'll be able to pay for it in two weeks. So you approach the car dealer and ask him to hold the car for you for two weeks, at which point you can make full payment on it.

The dealer agrees but insists that he will have to charge you $5,000 for the option to buy the car in two weeks for the set price of $100,000. You agree to the terms and give him a nonrefundable deposit of $5,000 (known as the *premium* in options-speak), which gives you the right, but not the obligation, to come back in two weeks and purchase the car of your dreams. The dealer, on the other hand, is obligated to sell you the car if you choose to exercise your option to do so. In this situation, you're the *holder* of the option and the dealer is its *underwriter.*

Consider two different scenarios that unfold during the two-week period. The first one is that, a few days after you purchase the option to buy the vehicle, the car manufacturer announces that it will stop making vehicles of this kind — the car is now a limited edition and becomes a collector's car. Congratulations! The value of the car has now doubled overnight! Because you and the dealer entered into an options agreement, the dealer is obligated to sell you the car at $100,000 even though the car now costs $200,000 — if you choose to exercise your rights as the option holder. You come back to see the dealer, and you buy the car at the agreed-upon price of $100,000. You can now either drive your new car or sell it at current market price for a cool $95,000 profit ($200,000 − $100,000 − $5,000 = $95,000)!

The second scenario isn't as rosy as the first. A few days after you sign the options agreement, the car manufacturer announces that there's a defect with the car's CD player. The car works fine, so the manufacturer doesn't need to recall it, but the built-in CD player is defective and not usable. Because of this development, the value of the car drops to

$80,000 (drivers like listening to their CDs, after all). As the holder of the option, you aren't obligated to purchase the car. Remember, you have the right — but not the obligation — to follow through on the contractual agreements of the contract. If you choose not to purchase the car, you will have incurred the $5,000 loss of the premium you paid for the option.

In a nutshell, that example is what trading options is all about. You can now apply this concept to profit in the capital markets in general and the commodities market in particular. For example, if you expect the price of the June copper futures contract on the CME to increase, you can buy an option on the CME that gives you the right to purchase the June copper futures contract for a specific price. You pay a premium for this option and, if you don't exercise your option before the expiration date, the only thing you lose is the premium.

Understanding trader talk

When talking about options, you need to know certain terms:

- ✔ **Premium:** The price you actually pay for the option. If you don't exercise your option, the only money you lose is the premium you paid for the contract in the first place.

- ✔ **Expiration date:** The date at which the option expires. After the expiration date, the contract is no longer valid.

- ✔ **Strike price:** The predetermined price at which the underlying asset is purchased or sold.

- ✔ **At-the-money:** When the strike price is equal to the market price, the option is known as being at-the-money.

- ✔ **In-the-money:** In a call option, when the asset's market price is above the strike price, it's in-the-money. In the land of puts, an option is in-the-money when the market price is below the strike price.

- ✔ **Out-of-the-money:** When the market price is below the strike price in a call option, that option is a money-loser: It's out-of-the-money. When the market price is greater than the strike price in a put option, it's out-of-the-money.

- ✔ **Open interest:** The total number of options or futures contracts that are still open on any given trading session. Open interest is an important measure of market interest.

Selecting option characteristics

Every option has different characteristics, depending on how you want to exercise the option and what action you want to conduct when it's exercised. Put simply, you can use options that allow you to either buy or sell an underlying security. You can further specify at which point you want to exercise the options agreement. This section lays out these characteristics for you.

Call options: Calling all investors

If you expect rising prices, you can buy a *call option* that gives you the right — but not the obligation — to *purchase* a specific amount of a security at a specific price at a specific point in the future.

When you buy a call option, you're being bullish and are expecting prices to increase — call options are similar to having a long position. When you *sell* a call option, you expect prices to fall. If the prices fall and never reach the strike price, you get to keep the premium. If prices increase and the holder exercises her option, you're obligated to sell her the underlying asset at the agreed-upon price.

Put options: Putting everything on the line

A *put option* is the exact opposite of a call option because it gives you the right, but not the obligation, to *sell* a security at some point in the future for a predetermined price. When you think the price of a security is going down, you want to use a put option to try to take advantage of this price movement.

Buying a put option is one way of shorting a security. If prices do decrease, you can purchase the security at the agreed-upon (lower) price and then turn back and sell it on the open market, pocketing the difference. On the other hand, if prices increase, you can choose to let the option expire. In this case, you lose only the premium you paid for the option.

When you *sell* a put option, you believe that prices are going to increase. If you're correct and prices increase, the holder won't exercise the option, which means you get to collect the premium. So when you sell a put option, you're actually being bullish.

Here are the possible combinations of buying and selling put and call options, accompanied by their corresponding market sentiment:

- ✔ Buying a call: Bullish
- ✔ Selling a call: Bearish
- ✔ Buying a put: Bearish
- ✔ Selling a put: Bullish

Looking at American options

When you buy an American option, you have the right to exercise that option at any time during the life of the option — from the start of the option until the expiration date. Most options traded in the United States are American options. You get a lot more flexibility out of them because you have the freedom to exercise them at any point.

Taking the European alternative

The European option allows you to exercise the option only at expiration. This is a fairly rigid kind of option. The only possible advantage of a European option over an American option is that you may be able to pay a smaller premium for this option. However, because of its rigidity, I highly recommend using American options in your trading strategies.

Chapter 14

Choosing a Manager or Broker and Trading Accounts

In This Chapter

▶ Investing through mutual funds

▶ Understanding master limited partnerships

▶ Working with a commodity trading advisor or commodity pool

▶ Opening an account and starting to trade

*I*f you're looking for ways to get involved in commodities, you have the option of hiring a trained professional to do the investing for you. As the number of investors putting their money into this asset class grows, more investment vehicles are being developed to satisfy this demand. Currently, plenty of money managers offer their services to help you invest in this market.

Of course, whenever you hand over your hard-earned money to a manager, you want to make sure that you feel confident about her ability to invest your money wisely. In this chapter, I look at some of the vehicles you have at your disposal to invest in the commodities markets, and I offer you hands-on information to help you select the most suitable money manager for you.

In this chapter, I also give you an overview of commodity exchanges, those important institutions that not only are responsible for setting global prices of all sorts of commodities, but also give investors a direct and transparent way to participate in the commodities markets.

Mutually Beneficial: Investing in Commodity Mutual Funds

A common way to invest in commodities is through a mutual fund. It may be the simplest way for you to get involved in the commodities markets because you're relying on a trained professional to do the investing on your behalf.

A *mutual fund* is a fund managed by an investment professional for the benefit of the fund investors. Mutual funds, by definition, can follow only a specific set of trading techniques. Mutual funds don't engage in sophisticated trading techniques such as arbitrage trades, special situations, long–short strategies, or distressed asset investing. These strategies are conducted primarily by *hedge funds,* which are similar to mutual funds except that they can engage in these sophisticated investment strategies. Most mutual funds follow *long-only* strategies, which is an investment policy based on the *buy-and-hold* principle.

Many different types of mutual funds have nothing to do with commodities. You can invest in stock funds, bond funds, currency funds, and even country-specific funds. But a number of mutual funds specialize in investing in only commodities or commodity-related products.

Plain vanilla funds are your run-of-the-mill funds. If you've ever invested in a mutual fund, you should have no problem investing in these straightforward funds. How do you get started? You write your check, purchase shares of the mutual funds either through your broker or directly from the fund providers, and voilà! Of course, I recommend asking a number of questions before you write that check. You can find these qualifying questions in the following section.

Plain vanilla funds are actively administered by a fund manager whose responsibility is to allocate capital across various subasset classes, to maximize the fund's returns. Generally, these mutual funds invest in commodity-linked derivative instruments such as futures contracts and options on futures traded on the major commodity exchanges in New York, Chicago, and elsewhere. Other mutual funds may also invest in companies that process these raw materials, such as energy companies (see Chapter 6) and mining companies (see Chapter 9).

Asking the right questions

Before you invest in a mutual fund, you need to gather as much information as possible about the fund itself, as well as about the mechanics of investing in the fund. You can get answers to these questions directly from the fund manager or the fund's prospectus.

Call the mutual fund company directly and ask for a prospectus. A *prospectus* contains a wealth of information regarding how the fund is managed, the strategies the fund managers use, and details on fees and expenses. It's a great way to start gathering information on a prospective fund. Best of all, mutual funds send you their prospectus for free!

Some useful questions can help you zero in on the key points of mutual fund investing:

- ✔ **What is the fund's investment objective?** Different funds have radically different investment objectives. One may focus on *capital gains,* where the purpose is price appreciation, whereas another may specialize in *income investing* by buying assets, such as bonds, that generate an income stream. Knowing the fund's objective is one of the first pieces of information to look for.

- ✔ **What securities does the fund invest in?** This may seem like an obvious question when you're looking at commodities funds, but a number of funds claim that their main investment products are commodities, when in reality, only a small percentage of the fund is commodities related.

- ✔ **Who manages the fund?** You want to know as much as possible about the individuals who will be managing your hard-earned money. Most money managers in the United States have to be registered with the National Association of Securities Dealers (NASD). You can get information on a manager's personal background by checking the NASD Web site, at www.nasdbrokercheck.com. Look for these key points:

- **Experience:** How long has he been a manager?

- **Track record:** What kind of returns has the manager achieved for his clients in the past?

- **Disciplinary actions:** Has this manager been disciplined for a past action? If so, find out more.

- **Registrations and certifications:** Does this manager have all the required registrations with the appropriate financial authorities to trade and invest on behalf of clients?

✔ **What kind of strategy does the fund use?** A fund's strategy relies on a number of factors, including the investing style of the portfolio managers, the fund's objective, and the securities it chooses to invest in. Some funds follow low-risk, steady-income strategies, while others have a more aggressive strategy that uses a lot of leverage. Identifying the fund's strategy right away is critical.

✔ **What is the profile of the typical investor in this fund?** The fund caters to the profile of its investors, which can be anywhere from highly conservative to extremely aggressive. You need to know what kind of individual is likely to invest in this fund and determine whether your risk tolerance squares with that of the other investors.

✔ **What are the main risks of investing in this fund?** Whenever you invest, you take on a certain degree of risk: interest rate risk, credit risk, risk of loss of principal, liquidity risk, hedging risk, and geopolitical risk. For a detailed look at a number of different risks, take a look at Chapter 2.

✔ **What is the fund's track record?** Although past performance doesn't guarantee future results, it's always important to examine the fund's track record, to get a sense of the kinds of returns the managers have achieved for their investors in the past. Most funds post their performance over a number of years; in particular, look at the key periods of the past three, five, and ten years.

✔ **What is the fund's *after-tax* performance?** Pay close attention to *after-tax* returns when looking at historical performance; they're a more accurate measure of the fund's performance — and how much money you get to keep after you pay Uncle Sam. Many funds use big, bold charts to advertise their performance before taxes, but these can be misleading because a significant portion of these returns ends up in the government's coffers after taxes are taken out.

✔ **What are the fund's fees and expenses?** Fees and expenses always cut into how much money you can get out of the fund. Look for funds that have lower expenses and fees. This information is available in the prospectus.

✔ **What is the minimum capital an investor must commit?** A number of mutual funds require investing a minimum amount of money, ranging anywhere from $500 to $10,000 or more. The minimum requirement may also vary according to the type of investor. Someone investing in an IRA, for example, may have to put up less money up front than someone investing through a brokerage account. Finally, many funds also require *minimum incremental amounts* after the initial investment amount. So you may invest $1,000 up front but then be required to increase your investment by at least $100 each subsequent time you want to invest in the fund.

✔ **Are there different classes of shares?** Most mutual funds offer more than one class of shares to investors. The different classes are based on several factors, including sales charges, deferred sales charges, redemption fees, and investor availability. Examine each class of shares closely to determine which is best for you.

✔ **What are the tax implications of investing in this fund?** Talk to your accountant to determine the tax consequences of any investment you make.

As with almost everything else in finance, investing in commodity mutual funds requires mastering specific terminology. These technical terms can help you talk the talk:

✔ **Expense ratio:** The expense ratio is the percentage of the fund's total assets earmarked for general operational expenses. This is the amount used to run the fund, and it generally lowers total fund returns.

✔ **Sales load:** Some mutual funds sell their shares through brokerage houses and other financial intermediaries. A *sales load* is the commission the mutual fund pays to brokers who sell their shares to the general public. The investor pays the sales load. Some funds don't have sales load; they're called *no-load funds.*

✔ **Sales charge:** A sales charge, sometimes referred to as a *deferred sales charge,* is a fee that the mutual fund investor pays when she sells her mutual fund shares. This charge is also known as a *back-end charge* because you pay a fee after you sell your shares.

✔ **Net asset value (NAV):** A fund's net asset value (NAV) is its total assets minus total liabilities. Mutual funds calculate NAV on a per-share basis at the end of each trading day by dividing the difference between total assets and liabilities by the number of shares outstanding. A mutual fund's NAV is similar to a publicly traded company's stock price on a per-share basis.

Mastering MLPs

If you're interested in investing in companies that are involved in the production, transformation, and distribution of commodities, one of the best ways to do so is to invest in a *master limited partnership* (MLP). MLPs are a great investment because of their tax advantage and high cash payouts.

The ABCs of MLPs

MLPs are public entities that trade on public exchanges. Just as a company issues stock on an exchange, an MLP issues shares that trade on an exchange. You can get involved in an MLP by simply purchasing its shares on an exchange. This is why an MLP is also called a *publicly traded partnership* (PTP).

Although most MLPs trade on the New York Stock Exchange (NYSE), a few MLPs also trade on the Nasdaq National Market (NASDAQ) and the American Stock and Options Exchange (AMEX).

The shares that an MLP issues are called *units,* and investors who own these units are known as *unit holders.* When you invest in an MLP, you're essentially investing in a public partnership. This partnership is run by a *general partner* for his benefit and, more important, for that of the *limited partners* (which you become when you buy MLP units).

The taxman only rings once

One of the reasons I like MLPs so much for commodities investing is that, unlike regular corporations, they're taxed only once. Many publicly traded companies are subject to double taxation: They're taxed at the corporate level as well as at the shareholder (individual) level. Not so with MLPs.

Because of congressional legislation, any MLP that derives 90 percent or more of its income from activities related to the production, distribution, and transformation of commodities qualifies for this tax-exempt status.

The income that an MLP uses to qualify for tax advantages is known as *qualifying income.* If an MLP can prove its qualifying income, it can "pass through" its income tax-free to its shareholders, who are then responsible for paying whatever taxes are appropriate for them. This is why MLPs are sometimes referred to as *pass-through entities.*

Curious to see how this tax advantage plays out in the real world? Suppose that you're in a 35 percent tax bracket. You invest $1 in an MLP and $1 in a corporation. The corporation needs to generate $2.20 in income to distribute $1 of after-tax profits to you. The MLP, thanks to its favorable tax treatment, has to generate only $1.54 in income to give you back $1 of after-tax profits.

This tax status gives MLPs a competitive advantage over other publicly traded entities when they compete for assets. An MLP simply doesn't have to generate as much cash flow as a corporation to distribute similar levels of after-tax income to shareholders — and this fact has two possible implications. First, if it wants, the MLP can afford to overpay for an asset and still generate healthy cash flows for its investors. Alternatively, it can purchase an asset at a similar price from a competing corporation but generate more cash flow to investors because of its favorable tax treatment.

MLPs are required to distribute all available cash back to unit holders on a quarterly basis. When you own an MLP, you receive a K1 tax form, which is similar to the 1099 tax form you receive from a corporation.

Be sure to inform your accountant of your MLP investments in advance, because most K1 forms aren't mailed out to shareholders until February. This gives you only a few weeks to account for the MLP income in your taxes.

Cash flow is king

The whole reason MLPs exist is to distribute all available cash back to the MLP unit holders, which has to be done on a quarterly basis. These factors determine how much cash is distributed to each investor:

- ✔ How many units the investors hold
- ✔ The incentive distribution rights (IDRs) created for the GP
- ✔ The difference between distributable and discretionary cash flow

The GP is responsible for distributing cash back to the LPs proportionally to their holdings. In other words, an investor who owns 1,000 units gets twice as much cash as an investor who owns 500 units in the same MLP. (But remember, this doesn't mean that the investor with the greater number of units gets to keep all that cash — she still has to pay taxes on this income, based on her tax profile.)

To promote the GP's efforts to increase cash flow for shareholders, many MLPs include incentives for the GP. Generally, the more cash flow the GP generates back to shareholders, the more cash he gets to keep. Although IDRs are different for each MLP, they're always based on a *tier system*. A typical IDR incentive structure for GPs increases the distribution rate to unit holders, as the following table illustrates.

Distribution Tier	Dollar Distribution	LP Payout	GP Participation
Tier 1	$0.50	98%	2%
Tier 2	$1.00	85%	15%
Tier 3	$1.50	75%	25%
Tier 4	$2.00	50%	50%

Using this tier distribution system, if the GP generates $1 of cash flow per unit (Tier 2), the LP gets 85¢ and the GP gets 15¢ of that dollar. However, if the GP is able to generate $2 of cash flow per unit (Tier 4), he gets to keep 50 percent of that amount, or $1; the LP gets a smaller percentage amount (50 percent, down from 85 percent) but gets a higher cash payout ($1) than other tiers. The GP is thus encouraged to generate as much cash flow as possible because he gets a higher cut of the profits. This example shows the incentive behind this elegant and sophisticated tiered distribution system.

The distribution of cash flow is known as *splits* because the LPs split their share of cash flow with the GP. Tier 4, where the GP participates on equal footing with the LPs, is known as a *high split*.

Therefore, it's in the best interest of the GP to maximize the cash flow to the investor. This point is important because the GP has a lot of discretion over how much of the available cash is actually redistributed to shareholders and how much will be used for operations related to the MLP.

Before you invest in an MLP, ask your broker the following questions:

- ✔ What's the historical payout?
- ✔ How much is cash flow?
- ✔ What is the GP's IDR?
- ✔ What are the operational activities?
- ✔ How much assets are under management?

Heads up! Risk and MLPs

Investing in MLPs comes with a number of risks. Here's a quick list of some of those risks so that you don't come upon any surprises when you get your K-1 tax form in February:

- ✔ **Management risk:** Because as a limited partner you have no say in the way the business is run, you're essentially handing over control to the general partner to manage the MLP as she sees fit. If you're not satisfied with the GP's performance, you can't do anything about it except withdraw your money from the MLP.

- ✔ **Environmental risk:** Many MLPs operate sophisticated infrastructures such as pipelines and drilling rigs, which are often vulnerable to natural disasters such as hurricanes and earthquakes. Any of these may have a negative impact on your bottom line.

- ✔ **Liquidity risk:** Because the MLP market is still fairly small compared to other assets such as stocks and bonds, you may face liquidity issues if you want to dispose of your units. Until liquidity increases in the MLP market, you risk not finding a buyer for your units.

- ✔ **Terrorism risk:** MLPs' assets often include sensitive infrastructures that may be vulnerable to a terrorist attack.

These risks are a few of the risks associated with MLPs, which is still a growing market. However, because of the beneficial structure and scope of operations of these entities, I believe they have a place in any diversified portfolio.

Relying on a Commodity Trading Advisor

If you're interested in investing in commodities through the futures markets or on a commodity exchange, getting the help of a trained professional to guide you down this path is always a good idea. One option is to hire the services of a *commodity trading advisor,* or CTA. The CTA is like a traditional stockbroker who specializes in the futures markets. He can help you open a futures account, trade futures contracts, and develop an investment strategy based on your personal financial profile.

CTAs have to pass a rigorous financial, trading, and portfolio-management exam called the Series 3. Administered by the National Association of Securities Dealers (NASD), this exam tests the candidate's knowledge of the commodities markets inside and out. By virtue of passing this exam and working at a commodities firm, most CTAs have a good fundamental understanding of the futures markets. CTAs are also licensed by the Commodity Futures Trading Commission (CFTC) and registered with the National Futures Association (NFA).

I've used these resources and found them helpful in finding the right CTAs:

- ✔ www.autumngold.com
- ✔ www.barclaygrp.com
- ✔ www.iasg.com

Each CTA has his own investment approach and trading philosophy. Before you select a CTA, find out about each candidate's investment style to see whether it squares with your investment goals. You also have to decide how much of a role you want the CTA to play in your investment life. Do you want someone to actively manage your funds or simply someone who will give you advice?

To answer these questions, you must first decide how involved you want to be in running your portfolio. If you're a hands-on kind of investor with free time to invest, you may consider investing on your own but keeping a CTA close by to answer questions.

On the other hand, if you don't have a lot of time or in-depth knowledge of commodities and prefer to have the CTA manage your funds for you, ask yourself a few questions to determine which CTA is right for you.

Consider these points when looking for a CTA:

- ✔ **Track record:** Web sites like Autumngold.com and IASG. com rank CTAs by their historical track record. I recommend that you take a look at the longest historical track record, which is the annualized return since the CTA began trading. However, it can also be useful to look at one-, three-, or six-month returns, as well as one-, three-, and five-year annualized returns.

✔ **Disciplinary actions:** The National Futures Association (NFA) maintains a comprehensive database of all registered CTAs, including a record of any disciplinary action the CTA may have faced. Make sure that the CTA you may be doing business with has a clean record. The NFA database that tracks CTAs is called the *Background Affiliation Status Information Center* (BASIC), and you can access it through the NFA Web site, at www.nfa.futures. org/basicnet. An additional resource is the National Association of Securities Dealers (NASD), which also maintains a comprehensive database of CTAs and other securities professionals. You can order a report on a CTA from the NASD by going to www.nasdbrokercheck.com.

✔ **Management fee:** Similar to most money managers, most CTAs charge a flat management fee. The industry average is 2 percent, although, depending on their track record, some CTAs charge higher management fees. These fees generally go toward operational expenses: paying employees, taking care of rent, mailing and printing marketing material, running a trading platform, maintaining a 1-800 number, and so on.

✔ **Performance fee:** Although a large portion of the management fee goes toward running the CTA's business, the performance fee provides an incentive for the CTA to generate the highest returns possible. This is the CTA's bread and butter. Again, performance fees differ among CTAs, although I've found that 20 percent seems to be a benchmark for most CTAs.

✔ **Miscellaneous fees:** Watch out for these fees, because they can add up really quickly — just like the miscellaneous fees you get on your cellphone bill. Ever opened your phone bill and found that miscellaneous fees increased your bill by 10 or 15 percent or higher? Your CTA may charge you for such items as express mail deliveries, check and wiring fees, night desk charges (a fee you pay if the CTA trades your account after trading hours), and maintenance fees. For example, if you don't maintain a minimum amount in your account — such as $500 — you can be charged a fee!

✔ **Margin requirements:** If you decide to open a *margin account* (as opposed to a cash account), you can borrow money from your CTA to purchase securities. Buying on margin gives you a lot of leverage (on both the upside and the downside), so knowing the details of the margin requirement is absolutely critical. (For more on using margin, take a look at Chapter 2.)

✔ **Minimum investment requirement:** Many CTAs require that you invest a minimum amount of money with them. This can be as low as $1,000 and as high as $200,000. I recommend investing no more than 5 to 10 percent of your investing capital with a CTA. This way, you diversify your holding to include managed futures, but it won't come back to haunt you if the CTA performs badly.

Jumping into a Commodity Pool

Another way you can get access to the commodities futures markets is to join a *commodity pool.* As its name suggests, a commodity pool is a pool of funds that trades in the commodities futures markets. The commodity pool is managed and operated by a designated *commodity pool operator* (CPO), who is licensed with the National Futures Association and registered with the Commodity Futures Trading Commission. All investors share in the profits (and losses) of the commodity pool based on how much capital they've contributed to the pool.

Investing in a commodity pool has two main advantages over opening an individual trading account with a CTA. First, because you're joining a pool with a number of different investors, your purchasing power increases significantly. You get a lot more leverage and diversification if you're trading a $1 million account as opposed to a $10,000 account.

The second benefit, which may not seem obvious at first, is that commodity pools tend to be structured as limited partnerships. This means that, as an investor with a stake in the pool, the most you can lose is the principal you invested in the first place. Losing your entire principal may seem like a bad deal, but for the futures markets, it's pretty good!

Let me explain. With an individual account, you can purchase securities on margin. That is, you can borrow funds to buy futures contracts. What happens if the position you entered into with the borrowed funds does the opposite of what you expected it to? Now not only have you lost your principal, but you also have to pay back your broker, who lent you the money to open the position. This means that you lose your principal and you still owe money, which is known as a *margin call.*

Now, because commodity pools are registered as limited partnerships, even if the fund uses leverage to buy securities and the fund gets a margin call, you're not responsible for that margin call. Hence, the only capital you risk is your principal! Of course, you want to perform due diligence on the CPO to keep the likelihood of the pool going bust as small as possible!

A good place to start looking for commodity pools is the Web site www.commodities-investors.com.

Ready, Set, Invest: Opening an Account and Placing Orders

When you're ready to start trading exchange-traded products, you have to choose the most suitable way for you to do so. Unless you're a member of an exchange or have a seat on the exchange floor, you have to open a trading account with a commodity broker who's licensed to conduct business on behalf of clients at the exchange.

The technical term for a commodity broker is a *futures commission merchant* (FCM). The FCM is licensed to solicit and execute commodity orders and accept payments for this service. Another term for FCM is *introducing broker* (IB).

Before choosing a commodity broker to handle your account, you have to perform a thorough and comprehensive analysis of the trading platform. You want to get as much information as possible about the firm and its activities. A few things to consider are firm history, clients, licensing information, trading platform, regulatory data, and employee information.

Choosing the right account

After you select a commodity brokerage firm you're comfortable with, it's time to open an account and start trading! You can choose from a number of different brokerage accounts. Most firms will offer you at least two types of accounts, depending on the level of control you want to exercise over the account.

If you feel confident about your trading abilities, a *self-directed account,* in which you call the shots, is the most suitable account for you. On the other hand, if you prefer to have a professional make the trading decisions for you, a *managed account* is your best bet. In this section, I go through the pros and cons of self-directed and managed accounts so you can determine which one is best for you.

Self-directed account

If you feel comfortable with exchange-traded products and are ready to take direct control of your account, consider opening a self-directed account, also known as a *nondiscretionary individual account.* With this account, you take matters into your own hands and make all the trading decisions. If you have a good understanding of market fundamentals and want to get direct access to commodity exchange products, a self-directed account is for you.

Before you open a self-directed account, talk to a few commodity brokers. Each firm offers different account features.

Specifically, ask about any minimum capital requirements the firm has. Some commodity brokers require that you invest a minimum amount of $10,000 or more. You also want to become familiar with account maintenance fees and the commission scale the firm uses. After you gather all the relevant information and open your account, you're finally ready to start trading and placing orders!

Managed account

In a managed account, you're essentially transferring the responsibility of making all buying and selling decisions to a trained professional.

Open a managed account in these cases:

> ✔ You don't follow the markets on a regular (that is, daily) basis but are interested in getting exposure to commodities.

✔ You follow the markets regularly but are unsure about which trading strategy will maximize your returns.

✔ You don't have the time to manage a personal account.

✔ You feel comfortable knowing that someone else is making trading decisions for you.

If these statements apply to you, you're ready to open a managed account. So how do you get started? First, you need to determine your investment goals, time horizon, and risk tolerance. Then you need to find out about any minimum capital requirements, commissions, or management fees you may face. When you have this information, you can move on to choosing a commodity trading advisor (CTA) to manage the account.

If you have mutual funds, the CTA is similar to a fund manager. The FCM, on the other hand, is more like a stock brokerage house. The FCM provides you with a trading platform, whereas the CTA actually manages your accounts for you.

A CTA is a securities professional who is licensed by the National Association of Securities Dealers (NASD) and the National Futures Association (NFA) to offer advice on commodities and to accept compensation for investment and management services. Before you select a CTA, perform a rigorous background check. Because a CTA is required to register with the NFA to transact with the public, you can find out a lot about a CTA by simply visiting the NFA Web site (www.nfa.futures.org).

You want to find out this info about your CTA:

✔ How many years of market experience does he have?

✔ What is his long-term performance record?

✔ What is his trading strategy, and does it square with your investment goals?

✔ Does he have any complaints filed against him? (This information is publicly available through the NFA.)

✔ Many CTAs manage more than one account. Try to find out how many accounts he's currently managing. If the number seems too high (more than 100), maybe your account won't be a high priority for him.

> ✔ Does he have a criminal record? If so, find out the details of any arrests or convictions he has. This information is also available through the NFA.

If you perform due diligence on your CTA and feel comfortable with him, you're ready to turn over trading privileges to him. How do you do that? You have to sign a *power of attorney* document. After you sign that document, your CTA gets full trading discretion and complete control over the buying and selling of commodities in your account. He then makes all the decisions, and you have to live with the good (and sometimes bad) decisions he makes. If you trade stocks, this account is similar to having a discretionary individual stock account, in which your stockbroker makes trading decisions for you. The main benefit of the managed account is that you get a trained professional managing your investments. The drawback is that you can't blame anyone but yourself if you incur any losses.

A CTA is allowed by law to manage more than one account and have more than one client. However, a CTA must keep all managed accounts separate. Thus, there's no commingling of funds allowed and no transferring profits or losses between accounts. A managed account differs from a *commodity pool,* in which your funds are "pooled" with those of other investors and you all share profits or losses. When you choose a managed account, make sure you get a CTA who will manage your account based on your personal risk profile.

Placing orders

Your trading account is your link to the commodity exchange. The broker's trading platform gives you access to the exchange's main products, such as futures contracts, options on futures, and other derivative products. Because the products traded on commodity exchanges are fairly sophisticated financial instruments, you need to specify a number of parameters to purchase the product you want.

Understanding contract parameters

The lifeblood of the exchange is the contract. As an investor, you can choose from a number of contracts, from plain vanilla futures contracts to exotic swaps and spreads. (I discuss these products in depth in Chapter 13.) Whether you're buying a forward contract or engaging in a swap, you need to follow specific entry order procedures.

Here's a list of the parameters you need to indicate to place an order at the exchange:

- ✔ **Action:** Indicate whether you're buying or selling.

- ✔ **Quantity:** Specify the number of contracts you're interested in either buying or selling.

- ✔ **Time:** By definition, commodity futures contracts represent an underlying commodity traded at a specific price for delivery at a specific point in the future. Futures contracts have delivery months, and you must specify the delivery month. Additionally, you need to specify the year, because many contracts represent delivery points for periods of up to five years (or more).

- ✔ **Commodity:** This is the underlying commodity that the contract represents, such as crude oil, gold, or soybeans. Sometimes it's also helpful to indicate the exchange on which you want to place your order. (This information is fairly significant because more of the same commodities are being offered on different exchanges. For example, the benchmark WTI crude oil, which used to be traded only on the CME/NYMEX, is now available on both the CME/NYMEX floor and the ICE electronic exchange.)

- ✔ **Price:** This info may be the most important piece of the contract: the price at which you're willing to buy or sell the contract. Unless you're placing a market order (which is executed at current market prices), you need to indicate the price at which you want your order to be filled.

- ✔ **Type of order:** A lot of different types of orders exist, from plain vanilla market orders to more exotic ones such as *fill or kill* (FOK). This info is an important piece of the order because you're indicating how you want to buy or sell the contract.

- ✔ **Day or open order:** Market orders relate to price, and day or open orders relate to how long you want your order to remain open. In a *day order,* your order expires if it isn't filled by the end of the trading day. An *open order,* however, remains open unless you cancel the order, the order is filled, or the contract expires.

Defining different types of orders

One of the most important pieces of information you need to indicate is the order type. This indicates how you want your order to be placed and executed. Table 14-1 lists the major types of orders, along with a brief description of each one.

Table 14-1	Defining Different Types of Orders
Order Type	**What It Means**
Fill or kill (FOK)	Use this order if you want your order to be filled right away at a specific price. If a matching offer isn't found within three attempts, your order is cancelled, or "killed."
Limit (LMT)	A limit order is placed when you want your order to be filled only at a specified price or better. If you're on the buy side of a transaction, you want your limit buy order placed at or below the market price. Conversely, if you're on the sell side, you want your limit sell order at or above market price.
Market (MKT)	A market order is perhaps the simplest type of order. When you choose a market order, you're saying you want your order filled at the current market price.
Market if touched (MIT)	A market if touched order sounds intimidating, but it's not. When you place an MIT, you specify the price at which you want to buy or sell a commodity. When that price is reached (or "touched"), your order is automatically filled at the current market price. A buy MIT order is placed below the market; a sell MIT order is placed above the market. In other words, you buy low and sell high.
Market on close (MOC)	When you place a market on close order, you're selecting not a specific price, but a specific time to execute your order. Your order is executed at whatever price that particular commodity happens to close at the end of the trading session.

(continued)

Table 14-1 *(continued)*

Order Type	What It Means
Stop (STP)	A stop order is a lot like a market if touched order because your order is placed when trading occurs at or through a specified price. However, unlike an MIT order, a buy stop order is placed above the market, and a sell stop order is placed below market levels.
Stop close only (SCO)	If you choose a stop close only order, your stop order is executed only at the closing of trading and only if the closing trading range is at or through your designated stop price.
Stop limit (STL)	A stop limit order combines both a stop order and a limit order. When the stop price is reached, the order becomes a limit order and the transaction is executed only if the specified price at which you want the order to go through has been reached.

Part V
The Part of Tens

Enjoy an extra mini Part of Tens chapter (okay, in this case, more like Part of Six, but still . . .) on the kinds of vessels that make up an oil company's fleet at www.dummies.com/extras/investingincommodities.

In this part . . .

✔ Monitor market indicators and apply the data to improve your bottom line

✔ Count down the top ten investment vehicles for commodities, including futures markets, equities, and fund investing.

Chapter 15

Ten Market Indicators You Should Monitor

In This Chapter
▶ Understanding the importance of market indicators
▶ Identifying the major indicators
▶ Monitoring the indicators regularly
▶ Applying the data to improve your bottom line

*T*he commodity waters can be perilous at times, and knowing how to navigate them is crucial. Keeping your eye on where the markets are heading — and where they've been — will help you develop a winning investment strategy. One way to identify where the markets are heading is to watch certain market indicators. The ten key metrics highlighted in this chapter provide insight into what the markets are doing and help you design and calibrate an investment strategy based on the market fundamentals.

Consumer Price Index

The *Consumer Price Index* (CPI), compiled by the Bureau of Labor Statistics (BLS), is a statistically weighted average of a basket of goods and services purchased by consumers around the country. The CPI is the closest thing to a cost-of-living index and is sometimes used to gauge inflationary trends. If the CPI is rising, economists — especially the ones at the Federal Reserve — start worrying that inflation is creeping up. A rising CPI may then result in an increase in the *Federal Funds Rate* (see the relevant section later in the chapter). The

CPI is sometimes broken down further into the *Core CPI,* which excludes items like food and energy. Comparing the CPI with the Core CPI can give you a good idea of how much consumers, who account for two-thirds of economic activity, are spending on commodities such as energy and agricultural products. Visit www.bls.gov/cpi for the latest data on the CPI.

EIA Inventory Reports

Energy traders are glued to their Bloomberg terminals every Wednesday morning (at 10:30 a.m. EST, to be precise), waiting for the latest inventory reports. Those inventory reports come from the Energy Information Administration (EIA), which is the statistical branch of the Department of Energy (DOE), and they detail activity in the country's energy sector. They include a summary of weekly supply estimates, crude oil supply, and disposition rates (consumer consumption), as well as production, refinery utilization, and any movement in stock changes. The EIA petroleum inventory reports may not get wide coverage in the press, but they have a direct impact on the price of crude oil and other energy products. Naturally, you'll want to monitor them regularly. You can find all the information about these reports by going to the EIA Web site at www.eia.doe.gov.

Federal Funds Rate

Perhaps no other market indicator is as closely watched by investors as the *Federal Funds Rate.* When the financial press talks about interest rates going up or down, they're almost always referring to the Federal Funds Rate, which is established by the Federal Open Market Committee (FOMC). This is the short-term interest rate banks charge each other overnight for Federal Reserve balances. When the Fed wants to stimulate a sluggish economy, it tends to decrease this short-term rate. On the other hand, if the Fed believes that the economy is overheating — and, therefore, subject to inflation — it increases this rate, which makes borrowing money more expensive.

Gross Domestic Product

Gross domestic product (GDP) is one of the most closely watched economic indicators. GDP is essentially a measure of all the goods and services produced in a country by private consumers, the government, the business sector, and trade (exports/imports). GDP, especially *per-capita GDP* (which essentially measures purchasing power on an individual level), is a good indication of the likely demand for and activity in commodities. The higher the GDP growth, the more likely a country is to spend more money on purchasing crude oil, natural gas, and other natural resources. Of course, GDP gives you a big picture of the economic landscape and may not necessarily identify specific trends. That said, solid and growing GDP is a good measure of economic health and is a bullish indicator for commodities. Theoretically, you can analyze the GDP of all countries, but I recommend looking closely at U.S. GDP, the largest economy on the planet, and the Chinese GDP, the fastest-growing economy in the world. These two countries are also the biggest purchasers of commodities such as crude oil and steel.

London Gold Fix

Gold is a special commodity because it's one of the only commodities that has a monetary role. For decades, many currencies — including the U.S. dollar and the British pound — were fixed to gold. Even though President Richard Nixon took the United States off the gold standard in 1971, thereby heralding a floating exchange rate regime, gold is still used as a global monetary benchmark. The Federal Reserve and other central banks hold gold bullion in vaults for monetary purposes, and economists sometimes use gold as a measure of inflation. Monitoring gold, both as a possible measure of inflation and for its monetary stability, is a good idea. Spot gold prices are fixed in London daily — in what is known as *London gold fixing* — by five leading members of the financial community. Precious metals dealers closely monitor the London gold fix and use it as a global benchmark for gold spot prices. You can also get an idea of where gold prices are heading by consulting the futures markets, specifically the COMEX gold futures prices provided by the Chicago Mercantile Exchange (CME/COMEX). Visit www.nymex.com for more on gold futures and www.goldfixing.com for the London gold fix.

Nonfarm Payrolls

As with the Consumer Price Index, nonfarm payrolls are compiled by the Bureau of Labor Statistics. Statistically, *nonfarm payrolls* include the number of individuals with paid salaries employed by businesses around the country. It does not include government employees, household employees (homemakers), individuals who work in the nonprofit sector, and workers involved in agriculture. Nonfarm payrolls include information on about 80 percent of the nation's total workforce, and this number is often used to determine unemployment levels. The nonfarm payroll report is released monthly, on the first Friday of the month, and does not include total employment; instead, it shows a change between the current employment levels and previous employment levels, as measured by the *new* number of jobs added. The higher the number, the stronger the economy and the more people hired by businesses — which all means that consumers have more money to spend. Although the link is indirect, higher nonfarm payroll numbers can be interpreted as a bullish sign for the commodities markets. Visit www.bls.gov/ces for more information on nonfarm payrolls.

Purchasing Managers Index

The *Purchasing Managers Index* (PMI), released by the Institute of Supply Management (ISM), is a composite index and a good indicator of total manufacturing activity, which, in turn, is an important barometer of overall economic activity. The manufacturing sector is a large consumer of commodities, such as crude oil and natural gas, and a strong PMI signals that manufacturers are doing well and are likely to spend additional dollars on commodities. The PMI is released at 10 a.m. EST on the first business day of every month. You can view the reports at www.ism.ws/ISMReport.

Reuters/Jefferies CRB Index

The *Reuters/Jefferies CRB Index* is the oldest commodity index and is one of the most widely followed commodity benchmarks in the market. Although commodity indexes have their shortcomings — for example, they track only commodities on futures contracts, thereby ignoring important commodities such as steel — they're the best measure of where the commodities markets as a whole are heading. The Reuters/Jefferies CRB Index tracks 19 commodities, everything from crude oil and silver to corn and nickel.

U.S. Dollar

Keeping your eye on what the U.S. dollar is doing is critical for a variety of reasons. U.S. dollars are the world's de facto currency, so most of the world's crucial commodities, from crude oil and gold to copper and coffee, are priced in them. Any shift in the dollar has an indirect impact on these important markets. For example, the integrated energy companies (the majors) have operations around the globe and often deal with the local currency in the area they're operating. Any shift in the local currency/U.S. dollar exchange rate has a direct impact on how the companies account for profits and expenses, as well as other metrics.

WTI Crude Oil

West Texas Intermediate (WTI) crude oil is one of the most widely followed benchmarks in the energy complex. WTI is a high-grade, low-sulfur, premium crude produced in West Texas. This light, sweet crude is traded on the NYMEX section of the Chicago Mercantile Exchange (CME/NYMEX) through a futures contract, which is widely quoted in the financial press and in analyst reports as a benchmark for global oil prices. More important, industry players use it as a benchmark for global oil prices. Of course, because the price of the CME/NYMEX WTI refers only to light, sweet crudes, the price of heavy, sour crudes is going to be different. Currently, most heavy, sour crudes are priced relative to their lighter and sweeter counterparts.

An alternative global crude benchmark is the North Sea Brent, which is also a high-quality crude that's produced in the Norwegian/British North Sea. This contract trades on the Intercontinental Exchange (ICE). For more on the WTI contract, visit www.cme.com. See www.theice.com for additional information on the North Sea Brent contract.

Chapter 16

Ten Investment Vehicles for Commodities

● ●

In This Chapter

▶ Investing through the futures markets

▶ Getting exposure through equities

▶ Uncovering the benefits of fund investing

● ●

*B*ecause the commodities markets are so wide and deep, you have a number of investment vehicles to access these markets. A common misconception among investors is that you can only trade commodities by opening a futures account. While the futures markets certainly provide an avenue into the commodities markets, you have other tools at your disposal. I list the ten most important investment vehicles in this chapter.

Futures Commission Merchant

Opening an account with a *Futures Commission Merchant* (FCM) is the most direct way for you to invest in commodities through the futures markets. An FCM is registered with the National Futures Association (NFA) and its activities are monitored by the Commodity Futures Trading Commission (CFTC). When you open an account with an FCM, you can actually trade futures contracts, options, and other derivative products directly through the main commodity exchanges. Your orders are sometimes routed electronically or are placed during the open outcry trading session. However, you should only open an account with an FCM if you have a solid grasp of trading futures and options. For more on futures contracts, check out Chapter 13; I discuss FCMs in depth in Chapter 14.

Commodity Trading Advisor

A *Commodity Trading Advisor* (CTA) is authorized by the CFTC and the NFA to trade on behalf of individual clients in the futures markets. The CTA is a registered investment professional who has a good grasp of the concepts in the futures markets. However, before you invest through a CTA, you should research their track record and investment philosophy. Find out what you should be looking for when shopping for a CTA in Chapter 14.

Commodity Pool Operator

The *Commodity Pool Operator* (CPO) is similar to the CTA in that she has the authority to invest on behalf of clients in the futures markets. The biggest difference is that CPOs are allowed to "pool" client accounts under one giant account and enter the markets en masse. The pooling of client funds offers two advantages: It increases the purchasing power of the fund, and it provides additional leverage. In addition, because a CPO is usually registered as a company, you can only lose your principal (in case things go wrong). In other words, you won't get any margin calls and owe the exchange money. Make sure to read Chapter 14 for more information on CPOs.

Integrated Commodity Companies

The equity markets offer a way for you to get exposure to commodities by investing in companies that process these natural resources. Some of these companies include large, integrated commodity-processing companies. In the energy space, these are companies like ExxonMobil (NYSE: XOM) and Total (NYSE: TOT) that have exposure to crude oil and natural gas in both the exploration and distribution phase of the supply chain (see Chapter 3).

In the metals complex, companies like Rio Tinto (NYSE: TRP) and BHP Billiton (NYSE: BHP) mine minerals and metals as varied as palladium and nickel. These integrated mining companies have operations throughout the globe. I cover them in Chapter 9.

Specialized Commodity Companies

If you want to get exposure to a specific commodity through the equity markets, you can always invest in *specialized* commodity companies. These companies focus on either one commodity or on one aspect of the supply chain. For example, oil tanker operators focus on transporting crude oil from Point A to Point B — that's the extent of their activities, which I uncover in Chapter 6. Other such companies include Starbucks (NASDAQ: SBUX) (Chapter 10), which focuses strictly on selling and marketing coffee-related products. These are good companies to invest in if you want exposure to a specific commodity through the equity markets.

Master Limited Partnerships

Master Limited Partnerships (MLPs) are hybrid investment vehicles that invest in energy infrastructure. They are in fact private partnerships that trade on public exchanges, just like stocks. This unique combination provides several advantages.

- ✔ Because the MLP is a partnership, it has tremendous tax advantages because it doesn't pay taxes on the corporate level, only on the individual level. It's therefore not subject to the double taxation that many corporations are subject to.

- ✔ Its mandate is to distribute practically all its cash flow directly to shareholders. It's therefore not uncommon to have an MLP return $3 or $4 per unit owned.

Check out MLPs in Chapter 14.

Exchange Traded Funds

Since they first emerged on the scene a few years ago, the popularity of *Exchange Traded Funds* (ETFs) has soared. And for good reason. They're privately run funds that trade on a public exchange, just like stocks. This ease-of-use has directly contributed to their popularity among investors. A number of ETFs have been introduced in recent years, which track the performance of commodity-related assets, such as gold, silver, and crude oil. But it's not just individual commodities that are now tracked by ETFs. Commodity indexes, such as the Deutsche Bank Liquid Commodity Index (AMEX: DBC), also have ETFs that track their performance. Turn to Chapter 12 for a complete listing of ETFs on the market.

Commodity Mutual Funds

Investors who are used to investing in mutual funds will enjoy knowing that a number of mutual funds invest directly in commodities. Two of the biggest such mutual funds are the PIMCO commodity fund and the Oppenheimer fund, both covered in Chapter 12.

Some funds seek to mirror the performance of various commodity benchmarks, while others invest in companies that process commodities.

Commodity Indexes

A commodity index acts a lot like a stock index: It tracks a group of securities for benchmarking and investing purposes. Commodity indexes are constructed and offered by different financial institutions, such as Goldman Sachs and Standard & Poor's, and they follow different construction methodologies. As such, the performance of the indexes — there are currently five — is different across the board. Most of these indexes can be tracked either through the futures markets or through ETFs.

Emerging Market Funds

Due to geographical happenstance, commodities are scattered across the globe. No single country dominates all commodities across the board. However, a few countries do dominate specific commodities. South Africa, for instance, has the largest reserves of gold in the world, Saudi Arabia has the largest oil reserves, and Russia has the biggest palladium reserves. As the demand for commodities increases, the economies of some of these emerging markets have been soaring. One way to play the commodities boom is by opening up your portfolio to emerging market funds.

Index

Dedication

This book is dedicated to my most steadfast supporters: my family. You have always been there for me when I needed you and have always supported me in every endeavor I've decided to undertake. I would not have been able to accomplish half the things I've done without your tremendous support, and for that I am deeply grateful.

About the Author

Amine Bouchentouf is a partner at Commodities Investors, LLC (CI), an international financial advisory firm headquartered in New York City that provides long-term strategic advice to individuals, institutions, and governments around the world. CI also invests directly on behalf of clients in a wide range of industries relating to natural resources, from crude oil and gold to natural gas and steel.

Amine is a world-renowned market commentator and has appeared in media in the United States, Great Britain, France, the United Arab Emirates, and Brazil. He is a member of the National Association of Securities Dealers and the Authors Guild and is also involved with the Council on Foreign Relations.

His family has been involved in the production and distribution of commodities for more than three generations. Amine holds a degree in economics from Middlebury College. In his spare time, he enjoys playing golf, traveling, and socializing with friends. You can stay up-to-date on Amine's perspective on the market through the website www.commodities-investors.com.

Author's Acknowledgments

I'd like to acknowledge the first-rate editorial team at Wiley for their input and assistance through every stage of this process. Thanks to Stacy Kennedy for helping launch the project early on and for her continuous input throughout the writing period. And thanks to the graphics department for helping me express my ideas and illustrate my points with the help of charts, graphs, and other helpful visuals.

Because the financial markets are so broad and deep, getting insight on all the different aspects of the markets is absolutely critical. I was fortunate that I could turn to some of the sharpest minds in finance for their insight on the markets. I'd like to thank Dr. Scott Pardee, at Middlebury College, for providing me with cutting-edge analysis on the cyclicality of the markets. I'd also like to acknowledge the contributions of Ray Strong, at Goldman Sachs, regarding all aspects of the energy markets. Thanks to Karen Treanton, at the International Energy Agency in Paris, for giving me all the vital statistical information on the energy industry. And thank you to John D. Phillips and Neil McMahon, at Alliance Bernstein, for their world-class research.

Kevin Rich, at Deutsche Bank, shared with me his knowledge of managed funds, and thanks to everyone at the NYMEX for their insights on the futures market. Additional thanks go to Frank Ahmed, at Bear Stearns, and Richard Adler for their general guidance. I also need to acknowledge the contributions of Elisa Castro, Heather Balke, and, of course, my agent, Mark Sullivan. Finally, I'd like to express my gratitude to my family, whose support was instrumental throughout this process.

Some others who provided very helpful input are mentioned throughout the pages of the book. I appreciate your help, one and all.

Publisher's Acknowledgments

Acquisitions Editor: Stacy Kennedy

Editor: Corbin Collins

Compilation Editor: Traci Cumbay

Production Editor: Kinson Raja

Cover Image: © Yurkoman/Shutterstock